THINGS
I WISH
I KNEW BEFORE

✓ I Retired

THINGS
I WISH
I KNEW BEFORE
✓ I Retired

ROCH TRANEL & TYLER BRAUN

INDEPENDENT CONTRACTOR OF MONEY CONCEPTS INTERNATIONAL, INC. All securities through Money Concepts Capital Corp. Member FINRA/SIPC. Investments are not FDIC/NCUA insured. No bank or credit union guarantee. May lose value. Money Concepts Advisory Services is a Registered Investment Advisor with the SEC. The Tranel Financial Group is an independent firm not affiliated with Money Concepts Capital Corp

Proudly printed in the United States of America.

ISBN Paperback: 978-1-717014-04-7

Cover Design: Michelle Manley
Interior Design: Ghislain Viau

DEDICATION

Roch Tranel dedicates this book to The Tranel Financial Group. *Eight Things I Wish I Knew Before I Retired* would not be possible without the dedication of this amazing team and their passion to serve clients. He also dedicates this book to his family, Kat, Jenna, and Alex. Their support has been a source of great inspiration and encouragement through the years.

Tyler Braun dedicates this book to his clients, whose real life experiences and personalities went into the book, and to the team at The Tranel Financial Group, who have helped to make this book a reality. Their drive for excellence and service has been invaluable. He also dedicates this book to his family, Amber, Carter, and Tatum, who remind him daily of what work, life, and retirement are all about—growing and learning together to live for today and plan for the future.

CONTENTS

ACKNOWLEDGEMENTS

It has been a great pleasure to co-author this book with Tyler Braun. We want to thank the clients who shared their stories and thereby helped us make the process of retirement much easier for our readers. This book is the product of the passion Tyler and I share with the thousands of clients we have learned from for over a quarter of a century. We are grateful for the lessons you have shared with us, and for the opportunity to share those lessons with our readers. —Roch Tranel

It has been a privilege to be a part of so many individuals' journeys into and though retirement. I myself have learned many invaluable lessons from the clients we have served. We feel passionate about sharing those lessons with readers who are just beginning their retirement journeys, and with readers who are well on their way. If not for the many unique people we have met, we would not have been able to write *Eight Things I Wish I Knew Before I Retired*. Our wish is that you, the reader, will be able to glean some valuable lessons that will aid you in making your retirement all that you have dreamed. —Tyler Braun

*Eight Things I Wish
I Knew Before I Retired*

IDEAL
VERSUS
REAL

Retirement brings out many emotions relating to your new purpose in life and your new retired identity. Look for the Personal Score Card at the end of each chapter, and tally them using the full Personal Score Card at the back of the book. This is an excellent tool that you can use to navigate the road of retirement.

The statements are designed to highlight areas that need further attention and development. Our goal is to help you identify the key components of your dream retirement plan.

Find Out Your Score NOW! »

INTRODUCTION

Retirement is a milestone. It's something you prepare for, something you're reminded of with every pay stub. As you have planned ahead, maybe you've focused on how you'll support yourself and what responsibilities you'll have. You might be looking forward to traveling or spending time with family. Maybe you even have a passion project to pursue. More than likely, though, you're apprehensive. You don't know exactly what's coming next.

At The Tranel Financial Group, we're here to help you figure that out. Over the last twenty-nine years, we've seen it all. Our team is dedicated to our clients' triumph in retirement. We are a family business, founded by a husband and wife team, Roch and Kat Tranel, who established The Tranel Financial Group in 1988 to help people reach their financial dreams. Since then we've grown into a dynamic team committed to our clients' triumph in retirement. Tyler Braun, Roch's nephew, joined The Tranel Financial Group in 2010, and in less than a decade, he has grown his portfolio's value to more than $200 million, a remarkable achievement that can be attributed to his interpersonal intelligence—his genuine ability to connect with people. Together, we're excited to present *Eight Things I Wish I Knew Before I Retired*, a guide to retirement based on the stories our clients have lived.

Retirement takes money, but it isn't about the money. We work as financial advisors, but much of our clients' success in retirement is about mind-set. If you have the right attitude and take these Eight Things to heart, you can find **triumph** in retirement.

In each chapter we'll address a different principle, using real-life examples drawn from thousands of clients' experiences, which will show distinct waypoints between *stress* and *triumph*.

 CONTINUUM – *Eight Things I Wish I Knew Before I Retired*

Stress ➤ Frustration ➤ Security ➤ Triumph

The personal stories in this book—each with a distinct background and perspective—will fall at a different point on the continuum above. Each chapter in this book will detail one piece of advice, one "thing I wish I knew." We hope you'll relate the stories we tell to your own circumstances, evaluate your position on the continuum with regard to each piece of advice, and use what you learn here to find fulfillment in your retirement.

When we talk about *triumph* here, we're not just talking about what looks good on paper or what society at large sees as success. *Triumph* isn't about being the most popular couple on the block and the envy of all your neighbors. We want you to have enough money to take care of your responsibilities, but we also want your life to have a broader purpose. Our goal is to help you find success that encompasses the monetary and the personal. When you achieve *triumph*, you recognize your value to the world and are able to work toward fulfilling it. It takes money, but it's not about the money.

The continuum we present is closely tied to the behavior we've seen. Here's how it breaks down:

Some people begin in a state of *stress*, without savings or goals for their retirement. In *stress*, they're often incredibly anxious. They might think, "I'm so far behind, it's not even worth it." They might self-sabotage.

Once someone in *stress* begins working, little by little, to attain his retirement goals, he might move forward along the continuum to reach a state of *frustration*. In *frustration*, some of the anxiety is relieved and self-sabotage is less common. Still, there's real difficulty. In **stress**, people attempt to save and prepare, but they struggle to find meaning in their work and personal life. Perhaps they're stuck in a job with little potential for advancement, or maybe they've stumbled due to circumstances outside of their control. Maybe they're nearing retirement age, yet they're unable to stop working due to outstanding debts or family circumstances. When people are in **frustration**, they see themselves as being tied to their current situation; they're unable to see beyond the now.

Some people come to us well prepared for their retirement, having reached a point of **security**. They've paid off their mortgage, put their kids through school, and accumulated savings. They know how much money they need to retire, and they've planned accordingly. This **security** is the good-on-paper kind of achievement that makes life significantly easier.

It's great to reach the point of **security**, but the happiest retirees do more. They know that retirement isn't just about hitting benchmarks. It's about using the resources you have to make a positive impact on the world around you. What that impact will be is up to you. You might find it at church, with your family, or in the community. You might take up a new hobby or reacquaint yourself with an old craft. Whatever your path to **triumph**, we're here to help you plan for it.

We've collected these stories and written this book to demonstrate the diverse ways to find fulfillment in the next chapter of your life. As you read, we hope that you'll reflect on your own experience and allow us to help you achieve *triumph* in retirement.

Everyone has the potential to reach *triumph*. We want you to feel confident and content in your retirement. In each chapter, we'll share stories to demonstrate how our clients have dealt with each of the Eight Things in *stress, frustration, security*, and *triumph*. At the end of each chapter, we'll ask you to use our scorecard to evaluate your relationship to that piece of advice and discover where you are on the path to *triumph*. Come and join us on this journey.

AN INVITATION

BRRRRING! AT 6:00 A.M., BOB ROLLS OUT OF BED, turns on the light, and begins the automatic motions of his morning. Bob has been getting up at the same time every day for decades now. His routine has become so ingrained in his body that he doesn't even have to think. But today is different.

Bob moves through the motions of his morning. He showers and gets dressed. He shakes his cereal into a bowl and pours himself a cup of coffee. He sits down at the breakfast table, and just as he unfolds the front page of the paper, his wife Betty walks into the kitchen and asks, "So, how does it feel, Bob, being just hours away from retirement?"

Bob smiles and shrugs. He's unsure how to describe this combination of emotions, even though he knows that Betty is here to listen. Since she took some time away from work to care for their two kids when they were young, Betty is still five to seven years away from retirement. She's excited to support Bob in his next chapter.

Bob feels the warmth of accomplishment, of course, but also the chill of trepidation. He's worked so hard to get to this point, but he is apprehensive about what will come next.

"I'm not sure," Bob says. "It's a little bit of everything. I don't know how to articulate it. It's overwhelming."

Bob feels a knot rising in his chest. Betty reaches over to squeeze his shoulder.

"You're not alone, honey. It'll be all right. And later today, everybody's coming together to celebrate *you*."

Today is different. Throughout the day, Bob's coworkers come by and shake his hand. When he turns over projects, his coworkers seem to make an extra effort to express their thanks for a job well done. As each piece of his professional responsibility gets placed into another's capable hands, Bob's stomach tightens, his mind turning to what the coming weeks will bring. How will he fill his days? How will others see him when he's no longer a full-time working professional?

Toward the end of the day, a calendar alert pings: *Retirement Party in Fifteen Minutes*. Bob looks at the file box filled with his personal belongings and makes one last sweep through his desk drawers before logging out of his computer. This is it.

Just for a second, the room spins a little. Bob feels a clutch of dizziness in his stomach and steadies himself against his desk.

What's next? he thinks. *Where do I go from here?* He sits up straight and takes a few deep breaths. He's accomplished plenty here and throughout his career, but now it's over. What skills will translate to the next stage of his life, and what will he leave behind?

Bob begins to stand and gather his things when he hears a knock at the door.

"Come in," he says. The door opens, and in walks his mentor, Gina. She smiles at Bob, the easy expression of a woman ten years into her retirement. Bob doesn't get to see her much now that they're not working together, but they sometimes get together for coffee. She's always been there for Bob, and he's glad to see her. Gina had taken time out from her busy schedule to help Bob celebrate his big day.

"Are you ready?" Gina asks with a knowing smile. Bob laughs.

"As ready as I can be," he says. She nods knowingly, and Bob is overcome with the realization that Gina has been here before, in this exact moment. She's felt the way he's feeling now. She looks great and seems happy with her life—she made it through.

"Well, let's head down to the conference room," she says. "Everybody's excited to give you the big send-off."

As Bob leaves his office, he still feels a flutter of nerves in his stomach, but as he nears the conference room, he can hear the chattering of voices inside. Bob takes a deep breath and walks in to a clamor of laughter and applause.

CHAPTER 1

FINDING PURPOSE

GINA'S STORY:
FROM FRUSTRATION TO TRIUMPH

THERE'S AN OLD STORY ABOUT THREE BRICKLAYERS. They were spreading mortar and stacking bricks, all doing the same actions, side by side. They looked nearly identical. One man, walking by on his way home, stopped and asked, "What are you doing?"

The first bricklayer barely glanced away from his work, shouting brusquely, "I'm laying bricks."

The second bricklayer looked up and said, "I'm putting up a wall."

The third bricklayer made direct eye contact with the passerby. He looked to the sky and said, "I'm building a cathedral for God."

The first bricklayer can barely see beyond his own hands. He describes his work as only the physical actions he is engaged in at that moment. He doesn't consider an overarching goal or a greater purpose.

The second bricklayer sees his work as a part of something larger than putting one brick on top of another, but his imagination remains limited.

The third bricklayer exemplifies pride, positive attitude, and perspective. His pride in his work motivates him to work hard, enabling a higher probability of success. His positive attitude propels him through moments of struggle; because he believes in his ultimate *triumph*, he can make it through difficult moments. His perspective—his ability to see the bigger picture of what he is doing—allows him to focus his energy on the most important tasks and provides motivation to excel. All of these character traits depend on a strong sense of self.

The fable of the three bricklayers illustrates the importance of attitude. Some people imagine that retirement is a static thing: you step out onto the porch, find your lounge chair, and settle in. Actually, like any other phase of life, retirement is a journey. It requires motivation and persistence. In order to have a successful and fulfilling retirement, you have to find something that gives you the third bricklayer's pride, positive attitude, and perspective.

In short, you have to have purpose.

Purpose is something that comes from who you are: your values, your traditions, and your passions. Finding your purpose is a personal journey; no one else can do it for you. This has always been Gina's motto.

We live in a society that doesn't necessarily bend to our will. Perhaps your purpose has to do with caring for your family; perhaps it is rooted in your community or your faith. Maybe your purpose lies in using your professional expertise in a charitable endeavor. No matter what it is, it has to be something that drives you.

Gina has always felt that her purpose has to be distinct from her career; it keeps her grounded. But when she talks to friends who are about to retire, she sees a lot of anxiety about what comes next. Retirement is a drastic change: the day-to-day of life radically shifts. Some people have worked in an industry—or even at a single company!—for forty years. They're likely accustomed to waking up at the same time, doing similar tasks throughout the day, and coming home to the same comforts at the end of the day. They might go out to the same restaurants on weekends with the same friends.

Retirement brings a change in day-to-day routines. It's natural to feel uncertain about that change. This is a time when life is about to be different from how it's ever been before.

When Gina was younger, she felt nervous when she decided to take time away from work to care for her kids. She thought, at that time, that she might lose who she was because she wasn't working accounts, managing others, and using her analytical skills. But that didn't happen. It was hard at first, but she found purpose in a different way. She still found ways to sharpen her skills and interests, and when she went back to work, it was all still there. Yet even with that prior experience with a major life change, Gina struggled at the start of her retirement.

At first, she didn't know her purpose. She started in a state of real **stress**. She had to move forward slowly.

From the outside, it looked like Gina had everything set in place when she retired. In some ways, she did; her assets were in good shape. But she didn't know what she was actually going to do with herself. And because she didn't have purpose, things really changed. She didn't know how she was going to spend her potentially lonely and unfulfilling golden years, and that worried her.

Gina had been saving—above and beyond what she needed—for a long time. Every time she made a sale, no matter how big or small, she invested a percentage of her commission, in addition to her normal payroll contributions. Her divorce was long settled and her daughter was grown and self-sufficient. Her finances were in order; she was ahead of schedule.

For years, Gina had spearheaded weeklong late-night pushes to meet ambitious deadlines. Thanks to her creativity and calculated risk taking, the company grew in unprecedented ways.

But Gina was also stressed during the last decade of her career. She took on more tasks than most managers do. She was very hands-on. Her employees were extremely motivated by working on her team, but her mental health had suffered. Toward the end, she'd developed a tremor in her hands. When she retired early, at age sixty, her family and coworkers felt relieved.

When Gina retired, she was financially *secure*, but at first, she really didn't know what to do with herself. She was accustomed to having meetings to moderate, calls to make, and performance reports to review. Without that structure, she didn't know how to proceed. Surely you can imagine the frustration of being in such a situation.

Gina loved the solitude of living alone, but until she retired, she didn't realize how much she depended on the structure of work to bring her into contact with other people. Once she retired, she kept to herself a lot—too much. She ended up spending all her time alone. Before, she'd always held engagements after work, but she stopped going to things like Bible study and book club because she'd always gone straight from work. She stopped going on her lunchtime walks because they weren't part of the break in her workday.

Looking back, Gina knows that if her friends had known what was happening, they would've been there for her. But at the time, Gina had no idea how isolated she really was.

In fact, Gina had no idea how bad things were until about two years into her retirement. She was feeling a little woozy at times and decided to go to the doctor. After a few tests, she learned that she'd developed type 2 diabetes. All those years of late-night work and takeout, plus her more recent inactivity, had taken their toll. Isolation had become a health problem. Gina's health had been good before retirement, but when she retired, she simply stopped keeping up with her well-being.

Gina had begun her retirement in what she thought was **security**, but she quickly ended up in a state of **frustration**. She had to make some real lifestyle changes. She had to account for extra medical expenses, as well as the need to implement new exercise and dietary regimens. It wasn't easy. And throughout it all, her daughter Amelia worried.

Amelia is Gina's only daughter. Gina—a single mother—and her daughter have always clung to each other; they're as close as a parent and child can be. But at that time, Amelia was living in Detroit, working as a project manager for one of the big car companies. She loved her career, but she wanted to help her mother. Amelia traveled back and forth to go to doctor's appointments with Gina. She called her mother every day. They even shared a health-tracking app to keep Gina accountable for all the changes she had to put into practice.

At first, Gina felt guilty for taking up Amelia's time and energy. She wanted her daughter to go off and be independent; she was single, living in a city she loved, and only twenty-five years old. Gina wanted her to go out with friends on the weekends, not come home to help her mother. But Amelia was a devoted daughter. She wanted to be there for her mom.

After six months or so of traveling back and forth, Amelia told Gina that she'd decided to move back home. She'd accepted a job with the county transit office without even telling her mother that she'd interviewed there! Amelia didn't want Gina to feel like a burden, so she'd kept it a secret.

Gina didn't want her daughter to abandon her ambitions; she wanted Amelia to focus on her career goals. But once Amelia returned, both she and Gina agreed that it was the right choice. The two had grown apart while Amelia was away at school. She was very ambitious, and Gina was proud of her daughter's accomplishments, but both of them were working hard and didn't make enough time to keep up with each other. They texted every day, but sometimes they'd go weeks without talking on the phone.

Once she moved back, Amelia finally confided that she'd been suffering from depression. She realized, after years of working hard during the day and playing hard at night, that she was using alcohol as a coping mechanism.

When Gina got sick and Amelia started visiting home on the weekends rather than going out, she realized that she had a problem. As she helped her mother to gain control of her health, she started taking stock of her own habits. Without ever telling her mother, Amelia quit drinking and started going to therapy.

Gina had no idea that when Amelia decided to move home, it wasn't just to help her mother. It was part of her recovery. Amelia wanted to take better care of herself while also taking care of Gina. A mother's illness became a daughter's saving grace. The two had been in a state of **stress**, but thanks to God's grace, they worked together to rebuild. Now, Gina's diabetes is under control. In fact, she's even working again—by choice, not necessity.

Once Amelia moved back, Gina began to feel a lot more settled and comfortable in her routines. She stayed on top of her diet and exercise. In fact, Gina's endocrinologist was so impressed by her switch to a vegetarian diet and her biking regimen that she connected Gina with an organization that helps newly diagnosed diabetics to understand their condition.

Gina started volunteering there, mostly giving testimonials at support-group meetings and meeting one-on-one with folks who were having a hard time adjusting. She was shocked to see how few people had good networks of support. There's a lot of shame that comes with illness. Some diabetics don't even tell their families at first.

Gina was motivated to find clarity and fulfillment in her life, so she worked for the organization as a volunteer. She kept speaking and counseling, and along the way, she saw little ways that things could be run more efficiently. After a couple of years of holding her tongue, Gina had developed a good relationship with the COO and one day, at lunch, Gina told her she'd noticed a few things that could save the organization significant money, especially on scheduling. The two got to talking, and the COO asked Gina if she would be willing to come on as a paid consultant. Gina accepted the offer.

Now, Gina is only working a couple of days a week, but she feels great about it. She spends plenty of time with Amelia, who's newly engaged and getting married in September. Gina adores her daughter's fiancé, and is ready to welcome a new member to their family. Finally, after a decade, she feels like she has reached **triumph** in her retirement.

Although it hasn't been easy, Gina is grateful for all that she's learned along the way to **triumph**. Gina now understands how important her relationship with her daughter is to their overall well-being. From that foundation of love and support, she reaches out to care for others who aren't so lucky. Gina's journey of purpose guided her toward a life of gratitude and service—and we couldn't be happier for her.

You may not be entirely sure how you'll find purpose in retirement—and that's OK. As Gina's story shows, finding purpose can take time and effort. The first step in this journey is to evaluate where you find yourself right now.

Think about your life outside of work. What brings you happiness and fulfillment? Do you find satisfaction in family, in a hobby, or in an interest that you haven't had time to enjoy in recent years? Whatever your purpose is, it will be something that sustains you. Using the scorecard below, rate yourself on the continuum of purpose.

⑧ PERSONAL SCORE CARD – *Eight Things I Wish I Knew Before I Retired*

Mindset	So Not Me	I'm Working Toward	You Know Me So Well
I measure my purpose through my growth, and through my impact on myself, my community and the world.	☐	☐	☐

IDEAL — REAL

CHAPTER 2

WHO DO YOU WANT TO BECOME?

D URING THE TRANSITION BETWEEN THE WORKING world and retirement, it's natural to be anxious about identity. So many people wonder, "Who will I be when I retire? How will I introduce myself?"

Change can be nerve-racking, but when it comes to retirement, it's often a good thing. It can be worrisome to wonder how others will view you, but after all those years investing in a livelihood, it's time to focus on *life*. Retirement is the time to enjoy yourself.

Think back to another transition in your life when you were nervous about what was next. It could the birth of a child, a big geographic move, or a career change. You probably felt a little nervous about redefining your identity then, too. But no matter how that change turned out, it gave you the chance to adapt and grow.

Think of retirement as another opportunity to be your best self. You can pursue new goals and describe yourself as *you* want to be seen.

In terms of purpose, there are two extremes of experience: working to live and living to work. Those who work to live use their jobs as a means to an end, focusing their attention on their families, friends, and communities. They see work as one part of a multifaceted self. For those who live to work, however, a daily profession can become all-consuming. They may not even consider retirement because they are so attached to the identity they've built in the workplace.

This "live to work" attitude can cause significant stress in retirement. People who experience stress when it comes to identity don't do much outside of work, and thus have difficulty finding purpose. Sometimes, they have difficulty retiring at all. They might have a pension, but not trust that it will be enough. For people who have struggled financially, giving up that security might be unfathomable; it might even seem foolhardy.

But in today's society, retirement is a necessary part of life. Because we live longer than our ancestors, we get to choose how we spend our golden years. You have the opportunity to choose what you do with your life.

The problem is, if you don't plan for your retirement, you don't necessarily plan out all the contingencies. You might let your rainy-day fund get low. You might forget to start drawing your required minimum distribution. You might end up leaving a burden behind for your loved ones.

How will your purpose influence your legacy?

PAUL'S STORY: THE LEGACY OF STRESS

Paul was a child of the Great Depression; as long as he was working, he believed that he could support his family. He was so focused on his work, he never even considered retiring. But then, when he was seventy, Paul had a heart attack at work. At first, he wanted to ignore it. He could barely breathe, but he didn't even want anyone to call an ambulance. His stubborn single-mindedness blinded him.

Thankfully, his heart attack wasn't fatal. Paul's coworkers' quick actions, along with his surgeon's skill, saved his life. But, of course, he couldn't go back to work right away; he had to recover and rest. He didn't even know when, or even if, he would be able to return to the factory floor.

The problem was, Paul had never planned on retiring. He had a pension and an IRA account, but because he'd never planned on using them, he hadn't felt the need to maintain much of a cushion. Instead, he'd always stepped in to help others. He had always been the first to come to the aid of family members and friends; whenever anyone else mentioned his or her financial stress, he'd been there to help. He'd believed he would always be working, so he gave a lot away.

Today, this view sounds crazy, but remember: Paul grew up in a different age. He believed in taking care of his community, and making sure his loved ones could stay afloat. So even though he was ahead on his mortgage and had a pension, things quickly became dire.

After his heart attack, Paul tried to renegotiate the terms of his mortgage to buy some time, save cash, and cover his extra expenses. But the bank wouldn't budge.

Paul wanted to protect his wife from the financial stress; he wanted her to be taken care of. He didn't want her to worry, but rather, to be able to stay in her home, in the environment where she felt most comfortable.

When the bank refused to negotiate, Paul had to tell his wife that they were in trouble. They ended up having to downsize into a duplex. The move was rough on both of them. Paul's wife tried to stay positive, but it was too much change for a woman of her age. Afterward, something in her faded.

It wasn't just the move that changed Paul's wife. It was the fact that her husband had never shared his trouble with her, and that he'd never considered the possibility that he might not be able to work for the rest of his life. Things don't always go as planned.

A few years later, the resolve of Paul's family was tested by the long-term effort to help their patriarch get through his final, difficult years. After Paul passed, and they came to terms with the fact that he had never considered building an identity outside of work, they became determined to live their lives with a focus on what truly mattered to them, not just live to work within the bounds of necessity.

It can be hard to hear about retirement mistakes; retirement should be a celebration, after all! But there's so much to learn, and it can be difficult for people who have struggled to tell their stories. You have to be thankful to anyone who helps, offers advice, or otherwise helps you to find **triumph** in retirement.

TONY'S STORY:
FROM SECURITY TO TRIUMPH

When Tony retired, he wasn't sure how he would build the legacy he wanted. To his family, Tony had always been a provider and a guide, but he wasn't sure exactly what he wanted to do when his career came to an end. But because of the struggles he'd watched his father go through, he knew he had to build an identity outside of his career.

When Tony retired, he was determined to build a legacy that went beyond what he did at work. He was already focused on his community; he served on church committees and cared for his kids, but he was always ambitious. He wanted to do more. He was in a state of **security**, but given his success in his professional life, he wanted to reach his full potential for **triumph** in retirement.

Tony went into retirement prepared. He planned ahead, seeking financial advice as soon as he had any savings. Tony and his wife, Carolyn, had two children, and they arrived at retirement in good financial shape. They had paid off their mortgage, leaving them with little in the way of debt. Because they had worked hard and advanced in their careers while still living within their means, they had a healthy emergency fund. Their portfolio was all set when Carolyn—a school librarian—retired in June, at the end of the school year, while Tony—an engineer—kept working until the end of that calendar year.

Always a go-getter, Carolyn quickly found a new routine to occupy her time. Soon after she retired, Carolyn started volunteering for the local historical society. With her master's degree in library science, she put her skills to work for a purpose about which she was passionate. She was excited to learn a new aspect of her field, and she loved helping others learn to catalogue and research. She was working toward a new purpose through a venture that allowed her to pursue new knowledge. It was a perfect fit.

When Tony retired, he wanted to spend more time with Carolyn, so he decided to join her at the historical society. He figured it would put him in touch with his roots and deepen his relationship with his wife. However, since he wasn't fluent in the language of archives and catalogues, Tony found himself assigned to dull tasks. He was sorting photos and taking out the recycling. He and Carolyn weren't even working in the same room.

At this point, Tony experienced **frustration** in terms of his identity. He kept at it because he liked being able to say, "My wife and I volunteer together," but he didn't find the work fulfilling.

After eight months or so, Carolyn told Tony that she could see he wasn't happy there. He confessed that he was accustomed to the challenge of designing complex projects and meeting clients' expectations. Working alone on tasks lacking a critical-thinking component wasn't fulfilling to him; it didn't align with his internal sense of purpose. The position could've worked well for someone else, but it wasn't the right fit for him.

As Carolyn and Tony began discussing his options, they reached out to their community. They got in touch with one of their church's deacons, who introduced Tony to a physics teacher who was looking for help coaching a high school science and engineering team.

From the very first conversation, Tony and the physics teacher got along well; they understood each other. Tony started going in to assist a few afternoons each week and learned how to teach the subjects he'd always loved. It was a new challenge for him; things like that keep one's mind young.

These teenagers were brimming with enthusiasm, just at the cusp of sophisticated scientific studies. With his lifetime of experience in the fields they were just beginning to explore, Tony was able to become a mentor to a diverse group of young people who could have a huge impact on the world—even after Tony was gone.

Through the process of mentoring students, Tony ended up learning a number of new skills; he learned about robotics, and he even sat in on some computer-science classes to learn new programming languages. He also worked as a career liaison to the most exceptional students on the team, helping them to shadow engineers at local businesses and apply for internships that would lead them on their own paths of discovery.

Even though he began in a place of *security* and mild *frustration*, Tony found *security* within himself from that work. He never would've guessed where he would end up, or thought such a transformation in identity was possible.

But through his involvement with family and community, he reached **triumph** in retirement.

When Tony passed away, his kids received sympathy cards form some of Tony's former students; it meant a lot to the family to know Tony had made such an impact on young people just embarking on their careers. In those notes, Tony's kids also learned that their father had made significant financial contributions toward his students' welfare; they'd had no idea. But as it turned out, Tony had decided he wanted to leave more of a legacy.

When it became clear that Tony and Carolyn would have a significant amount of money left in their IRA, even after cushioning their emergency fund, they knew that they wanted to donate that money. The science and engineering team was the cause Tony chose to support. When he died, Tony wanted his money to be put to good use, to help people succeed in the field to which he had dedicated his life's work.

At first, Tony figured that he would just leave the money in his IRA with instructions for his bequest. But as it turns out, that's not the best way to do it. After doing some research, Tony found out that bequeathed IRA assets get taxed; the team would've only received about 65 percent of what he'd saved. He didn't want to lose all of that.

So, Tony found another way to realize his potential for purpose. Since Tony would be required to start taking his

Required Minimum Distribution (RMD) at age seventy and a half, he decided to use that money to purchase a significant life insurance plan, designating the science and engineering team as the beneficiary. Tony bought a million-dollar policy and used his RMD to pay for it. Now, when Tony passed away, the team would get a million dollars. When he figured out how to make this happen, Tony was elated.

And yet, Tony decided not to tell anyone but his wife, Carolyn, who helped him make that decision. He didn't want anyone naming buildings after him; he just wanted the team to be able to keep doing exactly what it was doing. He didn't want accolades, just the ability to do something good and take care of his community. That's **triumph**.

When Tony first retired, he never could've dreamed that his drive and dedication would lead to such a contribution. But by living according to a strong work ethic and devoting his time, energy, and resources to serving others, Tony's impact went far beyond himself.

In Tony's case, his **triumph** didn't end when he died. Instead, through the identity he built in retirement, he also built a new legacy, beyond what he might have previously envisioned.

When you retire, you don't have to know exactly what you want your identity to be. We often say it'll take at least six months to get into the swing of things. Even if everything goes perfectly, there's a lot of adjustment.

*The key is to be flexible and maintain a positive attitude. After you've had some time to reorient to your new routine, check in with yourself. What would make you more fulfilled? How do you want to leave your mark? How would you rate yourself when it comes to identity? Are you married to your work, in a state of **stress** like Paul was before his heart attack? Are you feeling **frustrated** with your day-to-day identity, unfulfilled like Tony was when he first retired? Do you feel secure in your identity, ready for the next challenge and itching to make a bigger impact like Tony was after he became involved with the science and engineering team? Look at the scorecard below and place yourself somewhere along the continuum of identity.*

PERSONAL SCORE CARD – *Eight Things I Wish I Knew Before I Retired*

| | IDEAL | REAL | | |
Mindset		So Not Me	I'm Working Toward	You Know Me So Well
Work is just a small part of who I am. I identify myself through my hobbies and my happiness.		☐	☐	☐

CHAPTER 3

SMOOTH SAILING, DEBT-FREE

W HEN IT COMES TO LEAVING A LEGACY, DEBT-FREE living is the first step. While a small mortgage or car loan may not seem like a big deal, debt can be an anchor, holding you back from potential success. Any debt at all can prevent you from leaving behind the legacy to which you aspire. If something unexpected were to happen, debt can compound the problem. Like an anchor, debt drags you down. It wears away at your financial health and holds you back from reaching your goals. It can even prevent you from maneuvering out of the way when crisis looms.

There are some who retire with five or six years left on their mortgage and one small car payment, thinking that this amount of debt will be manageable. Other people end up delaying retirement because of debt that's accumulated over the years. No matter what relationship you have to debt, it's unlikely that you talk about it. It's a social taboo; people ignore it, hoping it will fade away. The problem is that it simply doesn't work like that.

Most people have some kind of debt, including a mortgage or a car payment. At first, taking out a loan is usually anxiety inducing. When you sign page after page to take out a mortgage, you can feel the gravity of taking on hundreds of thousands of dollars in debt. But very soon, as you start making payments and chipping away at a big number, you forget about it. You become accustomed to paying the bank every month, just like you paid rent before you purchased a home.

But getting accustomed to debt isn't necessarily a good thing. It doesn't make getting out of debt any easier. In fact, it can make it easier to accumulate unhealthy habits that further anchor you in place, keeping you from reaching *triumph* in retirement.

MARK AND LOIS'S STORY: FROM FRUSTRATION TO SECURITY

Mark never let anyone know that he had a problem with debt. No one knew about the massive loans that paid for his family's lifestyle. Because he had a good job in a high-earning field, he never had to explain extravagant purchases. Even his wife and kids didn't know what funded their vacations. Perhaps that's why it took him so long to get help.

Mark was successful in his work as a real estate broker; he was consistent, always getting promotions, raises, stock options, everything. His company grew consistently, and so did his commissions. His wife and the rest of the family were proud of him for rising to the top of a competitive industry. His younger brothers admired his business acumen and saw him as a role model; they never witnessed him falter.

The thing is, while it's easy to celebrate achievements, it's hard to talk about money in a candid way. We tend to speak in generalities and absolutes. We talk a big game, but maybe we don't actually live up to it in the way we'd like to.

For all those years, Mark was hiding something. Every time he hit a milestone in his career—every raise, every big deal he closed—he would reward himself. When he made partner, he bought a new luxury car. When he set a company record, he bought a boat.

It wasn't all for himself; he had three kids who he adored. He had them later in life, and they were very precious to him. Mark had always wanted a family, but it took him a while to find the right person with whom to settle down.

Mark didn't grow up with much money; he couldn't just go out and get new shoes whenever he wanted or splurge on frivolous things. But Mark wanted his kids to have nice, fashionable clothes and the latest tech gadgets so they'd fit in with their friends at school. He wanted his wife Lois to go get a manicure if she felt like it. He wanted the family to have everything. He felt so lucky to have a rich family life that he was always trying to do right by them.

The problem was, Mark just couldn't say no—to himself or to his family. Whenever someone in his family asked for something, he said yes.

Here's the kicker: all of Mark's major purchases were financed. Instead of using the money he made to live within the bounds of his bank account, he lived on borrowed means. When Mark would get a raise or a bonus, he would apply that money to the down payment for those big purchases. Rather than restricting himself to what he could buy with cash, he bet on his next windfall.

No one suspected what was really going on. Mark's family and friends assumed that Mark's success was covering all these expenses. No one likes to talk about the particulars of money. Why would Mark's brothers, or his children, have brought that stuff up if they didn't have to? Mark's family adored and admired him; they didn't want to offend him. For a long time, no one asked Mark what was going on. His brothers would visit Mark's time-share, or go out on his boat, never questioning his financial stability. But then, Mark's loved ones started to notice signs of trouble.

We all have neighbors who we see making improvement after improvement on beautiful homes, or buying new cars every two years. If you want something enough, there's always a way to justify it. In our credit card culture, it just takes a few clicks to get a whole new line of credit. If you only sign on the dotted line, you can fill a psychological void with material goods.

For people experiencing stress regarding debt, there's a sense of being owed something. They believe they deserve certain things: a car, a vacation, a new TV. They might live from paycheck to paycheck and still max out their credit cards. They see debt as a way of life; it's a crutch they use when they're not living within their means.

Eventually, as Mark's children got older and entered college, his wife Lois began to see signs of strain in her husband. She noticed his agitation peak when they were doing things that she thought were relaxing, like going out on their boat with the kids. Finally, Lois confronted Mark. She asked him, "Is there something I should know about our finances?"

The truth can hurt, big time. Lois was worried that even asking Mark what was going on would push him away, but when she finally confronted him, he came clean. He was in serious *frustration* with his debt. He'd gotten caught up in buying things rather than investing in his future; without thinking about it, he'd racked up significant debt.

He kept saying to himself, *I'll pay it off someday,* but he didn't have a real plan. He was waiting for the next big thing: an inheritance, or maybe a big spike in his company's value that he could cash in on when he sold his partnership. But he couldn't count on any of it.

It took a lot of work for Mark to get out of the poverty with which he'd grown up. Lois always imagined that her husband would've wanted to keep his finances in order at all times. She thought he valued solvency. But that just wasn't the case. Mark got caught up in convincing himself that he and his family deserved everything they wanted, and as a result, he wound up tied to a heavy, immovable anchor. He'd even taken on some bad loans because he fell for advertisers' schemes: six months with no interest, zero down, and so forth. He thought the deal justified the debt.

When Lois found out what her husband was going through, Mark was just preretirement. He was seventy, and planning to retire at seventy-two. He had kids later in life, so he was still paying for their college—something he insisted on doing, no matter what. At that point, he was almost at his wits' end. When Lois finally gave her husband the chance to come clean, he felt relieved.

Together, Lois and Mark took a look at what was going on with their finances. They knew that they were facing some serious changes, but they didn't yet realize the magnitude of the problem. Not only had Mark been taking out bad loans to make big purchases, he had also been transferring money back and forth on low-interest credit cards. They had $150,000 in debt! After years of wearing blinders and living beyond their means, they realized they had a big, big problem.

It's so easy to become complacent. With all the commercials and billboards trying to sell us the next big thing, it can seem like everyone's in the same situation of taking on debt after debt after debt. It's not easy to continually remind yourself that it isn't necessary or healthy to try to keep up with the Joneses.

At that point, Mark and Lois were paying more than 5 percent of their monthly take-home pay in credit card interest alone. Their behavior was affecting their future plans. They were committed to making sure their three kids could attend the college of their choice—whatever the price tag. They believed that education was the key to continued happiness and success, so they ponied up to take care of it.

Once they took a hard look at their debt, Mark and Lois focused on their habits and developed a plan for how they would begin to move forward. After so many years of acting as if money grows on trees, they told their children what was going on. Lois convinced Mark that secrecy wasn't good for anyone; if they were going to prevent such disaster from affecting their children, they would have to keep them in the loop.

Now, the family is in awe of Mark and Lois's discipline. Mark has stopped taking out new loans. He and Lois decided to move out of their home when their youngest child left for college, cutting their mortgage in half.

Lois was sixty at this point. For a while, she'd been entertaining the idea of retiring early, but after this wake-up call, she realized that it wasn't possible. She decided that she would put off her retirement until at least age seventy, putting in extra effort at work to stay engaged and challenged.

Lois's reinvestment in her career paid off: she was promoted to an executive-level position, which led to some stock options. It was a boon to their retirement, but Mark and Lois have a long way to go to cover three kids' college tuition. It won't be easy.

If they only had a mortgage, or if they had a mortgage and *one* car payment, their ability to pay for their kids' education wouldn't even be an issue; they're high earners. They're at ideal points in their careers to be taking on a challenge like that, with funded 401(k) and IRA accounts. And yet, they've found themselves in a precarious position. If only Mark hadn't spent decades trading in one loan for another.

Right now, debt is determining most of their day-to-day decisions. They're even considering selling one of their cars and carpooling to work. If they aren't able to discharge their debt, they won't be able to retire at all. Their debt is their anchor to the working life.

Today, Mark and Lois talk openly about debt and other financial issues. Their struggles have taught their children that for anyone, even for high earners, *any* kind of debt can throw a wrench in one's retirement.

As Mark and Lois's story makes clear, debt is a hindrance to financial freedom in retirement. Think about it: If you enter retirement with debt, you're beholden to the rise and fall of the market and global events. With outstanding credit card debt or a car note, you're affected by changes in interest rates, housing prices, and other kinds of volatility. There are far too many folks who experience significant levels of anxiety because of their debt. If you don't know how much your mortgage payment will fluctuate, that instability will affect every other aspect of your life. If you're held back by the anchor of your debt and you see a storm wave coming, you can't move; you can't react. Even if you're aware of the force moving toward you, you can't maneuver yourself out of the way.

Debt keeps you from **triumph** in retirement. Retirement takes money, but it's not about the money. You don't have to be a high-income earner to live debt-free. The key is to stay grounded. Live within your means and take stock of what you have. If you're jealous of your neighbors' new landscaping, or if you convince yourself that a new car will make you happy, you're deluding yourself. Fulfillment is something intrinsic, something that comes from yourself and the life you build.

Security takes discipline. It's tempting to see a commercial for a Caribbean cruise and believe that if you take that vacation, all your problems will be solved. You can tell yourself, *I deserve it*, but if you're trying to change your habits, you have to do a gut check. Credit card debt is certainly detrimental to your future financial health; a mortgage can be too. Keep reminding yourself that mass media makes big profits convincing you to buy things that you don't need. The best way to free yourself from debt is by living within your means from the get-go. It certainly isn't easy.

DAN'S STORY: FROM SECURITY TO TRIUMPH

Dan learned that it's difficult to stay financially sober in this world—especially when one is not earning a lot of money. Dan spent his whole career as a high school English teacher. He loved his profession and the satisfaction he got from working with students, but he certainly wasn't a high earner. He was always okay with living modestly, as long as he was doing work that mattered and that supported his no-frills lifestyle.

Still, it wasn't easy for Dan to become debt-fee. He worked his way through school and graduated with significant debt. In order to be a teacher, he went straight from college to graduate school, which didn't allow any time to save money to pay for it ahead of time. As a result, Dan ended up taking on significant student loans—loans which took him more than a decade to pay off.

During that decade, Dan took many precautions to keep himself from anchoring to even more debt. He never took out car loans; instead, he saved up and paid cash for his car, then drove it until it died. When Dan received his monthly credit card statements, he immediately wrote a check for the full amount. Eventually, when he purchased a home, Dan took out a mortgage, but even then, he made a down payment of 25 percent—more than twice the typical amount. It was always clear to him that a debt-free life was a stable and productive one.

When Dan was sixty-seven, and planning to retire at seventy, there was a year of bad rains in his town. That spring, the river overflowed and the city's sewer system couldn't handle all that water. Every house on his street flooded.

When that happened, Dan's basement was in dire straits. First, he tried to solve the problem himself, with a sump pump and a shop vac. No such luck—he had to wait his turn for the plumbers, who had to deal with more urgent cases before coming to his home. Though he tried to cordon off the damage with plastic sheeting, there was mildew and mold throughout the sheetrock in his basement by the time help was able to arrive.

Because the water damage threatened the house's structural integrity, Dan called in a contractor to assess the situation. The contractor advised Dan to tear out the sheetrock and floors immediately; that would keep the mold and mildew from spreading. The whole level had to be stripped down to its studs.

So, that's what Dan did—himself. Following the contractor's advice, he tore out the walls and floors, removing the sodden insulation and plaster. He rented a big construction dumpster and got it all done in a weekend. His friends couldn't believe it.

They told Dan, "Take out a home equity loan to cover all this mess."

Dan said, "No. I'm not going into debt over this. I don't want anyone to be able to take my house away from me." It was a convincing argument.

But other friends asked, "Why don't you just dip into your emergency fund? This is certainly an emergency!"

But Dan replied, "No—the damage is stable. I can save up until I can afford it. I'll wait until I can pay for it in cash so I won't have to disrupt my plans."

Dan wanted to leave his savings intact, in case something worse happened. He had seen friends fall prey to unexpected hurdles. He just wanted to be ready in case he got sick or a family member needed help. From watching his students, their parents, and his own family, Dan understood that there are emergencies more urgent than a flooded basement. Once he had taken care of the urgent parts of the problem, he decided to live with things being a little bit messy for a while.

When summer arrived, Dan did some additional analysis and decided to pay for the repairs (mostly the cost of materials, since he was doing the labor himself) by liquidating some IRA assets. Although the numbers might've worked out similarly if he had taken out a loan, liquidating assets simply felt different. He wanted to feel in control. Instead of being driven by debt, Dan sat in the driver's seat. He didn't want to slide back into a situation where he felt that burden.

Dan's repairs were a slow process. As he went through the renovation, he set himself a challenge: each month, he put extra money aside from his investment income and Social Security, depositing it into a savings account he'd opened. He wanted to see if he could he still reach **triumph**, even after a major financial setback.

Dan hadn't told anyone that he had a goal outside of repairing his basement. When he retired, Dan wanted to do work that would change people's lives. Although he'd been a teacher his whole life, he wanted to broaden his influence; he wanted to have a global impact.

When he refrained from eating out, or he carpooled or biked to work, the extra cash he saved went into his savings account, toward his global goal.

It's good to aim high, and it takes inspiration to reach beyond **security**. When Dan finally retired from his teaching career, he was 100 percent debt-free. He had loved his work, but he was ready to move on to the next chapter of his life, to put more effort into serving others outside of an academic environment. He had the strength of purpose and a determined identity that propelled him to continue to be of value to the world around him.

We all want to be of use and to be able to give back without feeling a sense of shortage. That's exactly what Dan had achieved. He was free of the anchor of debt, and he had peace of mind. He was free to pursue whatever opportunities came his way.

Dan was still ambitious. A decade or so before he retired, Dan had gone on a mission trip to Costa Rica, visiting a small town that was working to stimulate its ecotourism economy. He became friendly with the local residents and kept in touch with them when he returned to the United States. When the residents were planning the right allocations of farmland versus development, he helped to draft proposals and business plans so they could consult experts and make a more informed projection. He found a real passion for the work, especially because he'd never worked with such dedicated students of English. He even started taking Spanish lessons.

A year or so before he retired, once he'd finished repairs on his basement, Dan started planning for a big move: he wanted to purchase a two-bedroom cottage in Costa Rica so that he could be there to help the community in which he'd become so invested. His goal was to spend six months there every year.

It was a big goal, but he was just the sort of person to plan for something like that. He believed in frugal living and clear goals. After the challenge of saving while undergoing renovation, Dan accumulated enough of a cushion to easily maintain his condo in Illinois and take care of the flights, insurance, and rental fees necessary to set up his life in Costa Rica. He was thrilled.

The whole community was impressed by Dan's industrious retirement; he was really getting out there and doing something entirely new! Because he wasn't tied down by a home loan or other debt, he had the flexibility to pursue an unexpected passion.

Pretty soon after Dan started spending half the year in Costa Rica, his twin niece and nephew graduated from high school. As they developed more independence and specialized skills in their collegiate studies, they wanted to participate in their uncle's work—and Dan was eager to get them involved. During their first spring break, he flew them down to get the lay of the land and see where they could be of use. His nephew, an education major, jumped right in at the elementary school. His niece, an environmental engineering major, worked with the farmers to plan and build a new aqueduct.

To this day, Dan continues traveling back and forth between Illinois and Costa Rica, adapting his plans to the weather and the seasons. If the rainy season arrives early and stalls things down south, he flies home to Illinois. If there's a project that needs his translation or other input in Costa Rica, he can get there. Meanwhile, he's teaching a new generation to take on this important humanitarian work. His niece and nephew have continued their own endeavors in Costa Rica, establishing a group at their university to get more students involved. Every year, they raise funds to travel to Costa Rica for spring break—and Dan matches whatever the students raise. With no anchor weighing him down, Dan is open to whatever comes his way.

When you're looking to hoist the anchor of your debt, it can feel unrealistic to even try. But as Dan's story shows, it's never too early to talk about your debt and start working to reduce it. Everyone's road to *triumph* is different, but we all have the chance to make an impact through the legacy we leave.

We want everyone to be open to the possibility of a richer life in retirement—and that means being debt-free. Without the anchor of debt weighing you down, you can celebrate your successes and retire in **triumph**.

You deserve freedom from insecurity, not material objects that require contracts and interest payments. How can you get there? Is it adding a little extra to each mortgage payment? Is it cutting out something you don't need?

Wherever you are right now, you have the chance to move toward **triumph**. *It may take some work, and it may not be comfortable at first, but everyone has an opportunity to move forward.*

Take a minute to rate yourself on debt according to the scorecard below. Have you gotten caught up in material things—perhaps more so than you can afford? Lay all of your debt out in front of you and look at it. Now, are you ready to pay cash for a property in a warm climate? Or is it time to instill some discipline to move yourself forward toward smooth sailing, anchors aweigh?

No matter what state you find yourself in, it's time to take stock and be realistic: Are you stuck because of your debt? Rate yourself on the scorecard below.

8 PERSONAL SCORE CARD – *Eight Things I Wish I Knew Before I Retired*

| | IDEAL | REAL | | |
Mindset	So Not Me	I'm Working Toward	You Know Me So Well
I am at peace and happy where I am in life. I rarely think about money, knowing I am in a good place.	☐	☐	☐

CHAPTER 4

HOW MUCH IS ENOUGH?

SOMETIMES THE ROAD TO RETIREMENT FEELS LIKE it will never end. It takes a lot of work to reach that ultimate destination: stacked files of account statements, nights crunching numbers at the kitchen table, spreadsheets and legal pads, late-night worries whispered aloud. Once the time comes, it can be hard to let go.

No matter how many times you go over the details, you might still feel apprehensive. It's natural to feel unsure about the future, to think, *Am I retiring too soon? Could I have saved more?*

In truth, it's difficult to know exactly when to pull the trigger and retire. That's because retirement is all about perspective. Having enough is more of a mind-set than a state of being. You have to know what you want, then work toward it.

Retirement isn't a one-size-fits-all arrangement; everyone's number is different. Family, geography, and plenty of other factors contribute to the landscape of each individual's retirement necessities. Of course, there are people who use that complex landscape as an excuse for ignorance, letting the nuances intimidate them. But ignorance isn't bliss. If you don't know where you're going, how can you get there?

LINDA'S STORY: FROM SECURITY TO STRESS

Linda has had a hard time preparing for retirement. At one point, earlier in her life, Linda was **secure** in her plans, focused on what lay ahead. Now, she's moved into a state of **stress**. A number of factors have contributed to her backsliding, but the root of the problem is that Linda hasn't set a financial goal. Without a specific milestone in mind, she can't make the right decisions.

Fifteen years ago, Linda seemed like she was in a good place. She and her husband, Jerry, had started planning for their financial future when they were in their forties. They both had good jobs: Linda was an engineer at a pharmaceutical company, and Jerry was a high school teacher and basketball coach. Jerry had a pension; Linda had been putting money into her 401(k). They hadn't accumulated much of an IRA yet, but they were making progress in saving for their daughter's college. There was more Jerry and Linda could do—there always is—but they seemed to be on the right track.

Then came the accident. Jerry was on the way to a game when a semi skidded into the school bus, running it off the road. A dozen students were badly injured, and both Jerry and the bus driver were killed.

At that point, Linda's sister and mother took time off of work to help Linda and her daughter, Lisa. Her family wanted Linda and Lisa to have time to grieve without worrying about the little things. They helped with the shopping and the cleaning, keeping Linda afloat during the darkest days of her grief.

Part of Linda's process of mourning was seeking restitution for Jerry's death. Apparently, the semi driver had tested positive for amphetamines. As soon as that fact became clear, Linda filed a wrongful death lawsuit against the trucking company. Her lawyers told her the case was cut and dried, so Linda felt comfortable cutting back on her hours at work. She wanted to be home more with Lisa and spend time at church, another community that was providing her with emotional and spiritual support in her time of need.

Throughout this time, Linda's family was concerned, but they also had to be sensitive. Linda had just been widowed, suddenly and horrifically. Her family worried that it wasn't a great idea for Linda to decrease her income, but Linda kept insisting everything would be taken care of as soon as she won the lawsuit.

It's a risky bet to count on future earnings to take care of debts. Linda's situation could be another kind of bad bet. What if the lawsuit didn't pan out?

Family and church provided emotional support for Linda and Lisa throughout the legal proceedings. It took eighteen months for the case to go before a judge, and when it did, it was tried in the same county where the trucking company was headquartered. Later, they found out that the presiding judge was friends with the trucking company's CEO. Linda ended up losing what should've been a simple case with a significant payout. After all the anguish and anticipation, she came up empty-handed.

During the months between the accident and the ruling, Linda had been working only twenty hours per week. She'd burned through her emergency money. She'd stopped adding to Lisa's college fund. Financially, she'd stalled completely in a state bordering between *frustration* and **stress**.

When Linda's family sat her down to tell her, "You have to get your act together financially," they were shocked to hear Linda say, "I'm getting married again."

Linda's family knew that she had been spending a lot of time with a man she'd met at church. The two were excited to make their life together, and Linda's parents, sister, and other family members wanted to be excited for her; she'd been through so much turmoil. But the family members had their doubts.

During Linda's engagement, her parents and sister tried to talk to her more about her finances. But she was doe-eyed, and they felt incapable of bursting her bubble. It wasn't until after the wedding that they had a frank discussion about Linda's finances.

Linda got married about two years after the accident. After she and her new husband returned from their honeymoon in the Caribbean, Linda's sister invited her to lunch so that they could talk alone. For months, Linda's sister had tried to tell herself that Linda was okay, that Linda and her husband must have had things figured out. But as a pragmatist, Linda's sister was at her wits' end with worry. She couldn't stop thinking about her niece, Lisa, who was a freshman in high school at that point. College tuition was looming on the horizon. How would her sister make sure Lisa could pursue her dreams? What if Linda's mistakes impacted her daughter's ability to find success in the future?

When Linda and her sister sat down, Linda looked tan and happy from a week at the beach. But when she started telling her sister about her plans to remodel her basement, her sister could feel herself getting angry. What was Linda doing? Why would she sabotage herself like this?

Linda had gone back to work full-time, but she couldn't afford a major home-construction project while still putting money away for future needs. Her husband was a car salesman, working mostly on commission. From what clues her sister had gathered, it seemed like he didn't have much in the way of savings. Linda had paid for most of the wedding expenses herself. Her sister tried to stay calm as she asked outright, "Where's the money coming from?"

Linda told her sister the funding for the remodel came from her 401(k). She'd slowed her contributions "just for now," she insisted, claiming that the new basement would increase the value of the house, and that it would pay off in the long run. Her sister was terrified for her.

The one positive moment of that tense lunch came when Linda assured her sister that she'd resumed contributions to Lisa's college fund. Everything was back on track there—a huge relief. But when it came to preparing for her own future, things were effectively stalled.

Money can be so emotional; it's all tied up in the events of our lives. Grief might have clouded Linda's judgment. She tried to hide her concern. Linda's sister could see the turmoil in Linda's eyes, so she helped her reach out to a professional, someone she would trust to help her see how her decisions could affect her future. Together, they went to the advisor, but little changed.

Linda and her husband went all out on the basement remodel: a huge game room, fiber-optic cables, everything. And then, just when Linda's family was starting to breathe a sigh of relief, they got to work on the backyard! Linda agreed to consider getting some financial advice, but she didn't appear to be listening to anyone else.

At this point, Linda and her husband are in their late fifties. They have taken out a home equity loan for the landscaping, adding another five years to their mortgage. It's not clear when—or even *if*—Linda will be able to retire.

The bright spot in this stressful situation is Lisa. Lisa is in college now; she's all taken care of, thanks to her father's early planning, but her mother still hasn't come to her senses.

When you get as far behind as Linda is, it's easy to think, *Why try?* You self-sabotage. You know the train is going to crash, so you don't even attempt to pull the emergency brake to stop it. For whatever reason, be it upbringing or circumstance, some people seem destined to self-destruct. In these cases, friends and family can do their best to minimize the collateral damage, but sometimes there's not much that can be done. In the end, so much comes down to personal judgment.

ROBERT'S STORY:
FROM STRESS TO SECURITY

Robert worked for forty years as a custodian at a large corporation. He spent all that time doing hard manual labor, and by the time he was sixty, he had bad arthritis in his hip. Work became extremely difficult and painful; doing anything physical after the end of the long workday was out of the question. He would come home, lie down, and not get up again until he went to work the next morning. He was getting by, but he was in a state of *frustration*.

After Robert's wife passed away from cancer, he felt like he'd run into a brick wall. He was full of grief, in addition to suffering due to his physical ailments. He decided that he wanted to know exactly when he could retire so that he could put that date on the calendar and work toward it.

With his daughter's help, Robert realized that he could live off of his IRA's dividends alone for a few years, and then start taking distributions from Social Security down the road. He was elated. He started planning more on his own. He discovered that if he sold his house and moved into a condo, he could use some of the savings to help his daughter save for *her* kids' college tuition. It was an unbelievably kind thought. With all of that taken into account, it would be possible for him to retire at age sixty-two.

If only he'd made it there. Six months before he was to hit his goal, Robert had a bad fall. He slipped at home and broke his hip. He had surgery, followed by a long recovery, and then there were complications. At first, he was determined to get back to work, but it proved to be impossible.

During that time, his daughter was effectively working double shifts; she would go straight from the office to the hospital, and then return home to sleep. She didn't have a second to breathe. She also had young kids, who her husband watched while she was running around. Her family members pitched in where they could. That's the thing about family: you're there for each other.

When everything else fell through, Robert was lucky to have family to fall back on. After the fall and broken hip, Robert was approved for short-term government disability, but because his fall occurred at home, the company denied his permanent disability claim. Even though the fall was probably caused, and certainly worsened, by the arthritis he developed *at work*, the company wouldn't pay.

Robert's family members were thankful they'd already established a financial plan. They were clear about Robert's finances and priorities. After Robert lost his appeal to the company's board of trustees, the family was ready with a fully developed plan to make sure Robert could have the retirement he deserved.

As soon as Robert entered a rehab facility, the family started the process of selling his home so that he could move into a fully accessible apartment. The house sold more quickly than they'd anticipated, thanks to Robert's upkeep and the good school district. Because it sold so quickly, Robert moved in with his daughter and her family temporarily. His daughter had thought it would be a difficult transition—her kids were just four and six—but it turned out to be a gift to all of them. Robert's son-in-law liked having him around to watch baseball with, and Robert was such a calming presence for the kids. More than that, the big, bustling family life motivated him to do the hard work necessary for his recovery. He wanted to be able to play with the grandkids, go to their games, and provide for their future in whatever way he could.

Robert ended up living with his daughter for three years. He was almost sixty-four when he found a condo he loved and bought it. In the meantime, he'd really tightened his belt. He worried about future maintenance care for his arthritis, so he set up an extra medical fund, using his first year's expenses as a guide. Once he was back on his feet, he learned to cook. He wasn't useless in the kitchen before, but he started to have fun with it. It saved him money and improved his health.

For the next thirteen years, until he passed, Robert lived a happy life in his condo. But even ten years after having moved in, he'd bristle at any mention of the company he'd worked for. He'd say, "To the company, a worker is just a number. They'll never take care of you."

Robert's story truly demonstrates that family and community can come together to accomplish what money may not be able to. At the end of his life, Robert was able to set new goals and chart his own path.

For him, the money was a means to an end—not who he was. Robert demonstrated to his grandchildren that family is the most important thing. If you have the support of people you love, everything else will follow.

Perhaps Linda will have to make compromises in order to retire. Perhaps she'll end up living on less. But maybe that decision will open up a new door. If you had a dream to pursue, what would you do to get there? Could your concept of "enough" adapt to a sense of gratitude for what you have?

*How much money is enough for you to retire? The answer depends on what your goals are, how you plan to spend your time, and how much flexibility you've built in to your lifestyle. If you're willing to take things as they come, you're far more likely to find personal **triumph** in retirement. Do you know what you need? What do you want to achieve?*

*Take a moment to think through your goals. What do you want to accomplish? What are the monetary resources necessary to reach those goals? Do you have them in place already? If not, what will it take to get there? Are you in a state of **stress**, like Linda? Are you in transition, facing* *unforeseen obstacles like Robert? Or are you closer to a state of* **triumph***?*

Considering your own sense of "How Much Is Enough," rate yourself according to the scorecard below.

PERSONAL SCORE CARD – *Eight Things I Wish I Knew Before I Retired*

	IDEAL	REAL		
Mindset		So Not Me	I'm Working Toward	You Know Me So Well
Days don't always go as planned, but I have a great life plan to allow for ups and downs.		☐	☐	☐

CHAPTER 5

INSULATING FROM INSECURITY

A<small>T A CERTAIN POINT IN YOUR CAREER, YOU'VE</small> probably arrived at a feeling of comfort, but it rarely comes easily. *Security* isn't a given, and it certainly doesn't occur overnight.

Early on, you might've spent Saturday mornings clipping coupons at the kitchen table. For many families, having young kids means keeping belts tightened and constantly looking for ways to shave a dollar off the bills. It's all about the daily habits that compound over time to achieve results. Some people are real whizzes at trimming the pocketbook. They know the tricks. When their children are young, they wait for big sales to buy baby wipes in bulk; once their kids are in school, they stockpile their cabinets with pencils, binders, and notebook paper. For bigger investments like computers or cars, they tend to buy things secondhand and perform repairs themselves.

As retirement gets closer, many good savers get to the point where they're more comfortable going out for a nice meal every once in a while. They don't feel uneasy about staying in a hotel when they go to visit family a few hours away. They might even take a big vacation.

Along the way, most people experience small bumps in the road. Maybe one of their children got hurt and needed surgery, or one of their parents required some extra help covering home health care. But for people who've been blessed with good luck overall, it becomes easier to save more and more as the years go by.

Still, everyone fears the unexpected. What if you get injured? What if something happens and you need to help support one of your children? As soon as you begin to entertain these thoughts, they multiply, intensifying your anxiety until your head spins from all the dire possibilities you've concocted.

Many people come to us and ask, "What if we aren't as prepared as we think we are?" Even if they keep their emergency fund stocked, they're worried that losing the extra cushion of a salary coming in will leave them more vulnerable to unforeseen expenses.

If you want to be prepared, it's important to build extra flexibility into your plans. Don't just focus on the big number; keep your portfolio malleable so that you can adapt to new situations.

For many people, the prospect of not receiving a paycheck from an employer can be terrifying. Some respond to that fear with rigidity. They believe that comprehensive planning will ensure that no surprises will catch them off guard. Unfortunately, this isn't always the case. None of us can predict the future or prevent unexpected events.

For many people whose careers are winding down, the focus is on the big number: the portfolio sum that means "enough." But it also takes time to organize finances to account for the inevitability of change.

Perhaps if more people considered contingencies sooner, they might come to understand that retirement is about more than an account balance; it's about a philosophy of life, an attitude toward the changes that inevitably occur. Sadly, far too many retirees learn that lesson the hard way.

In planning, a great number of people draw up all kinds of scenarios to project exactly how each year will play out. They build out spreadsheets with projections for favorable, average, and unfavorable conditions. They set specific guidelines and make predictions accordingly, insisting on their views and refusing to accept some of the unavoidable risks. They might say things like, "I'll never dip into my emergency fund before age seventy," or "I'll never need a supplemental insurance policy," refusing to build in more cushion than their own analysis shows to be necessary. They simply believe that their numbers will carry them through.

The temptation to make a rigid plan is understandable. You want things to go well, and making a plan can help you *feel* like things are under control. Risk simply feels more present when you're looking at retirement. It's tempting to think that if you plan well enough, playing out scenario after scenario, you can plot a straight-and-narrow path and follow it.

If only!

The problem is, life happens. Things change—for better *and* for worse. It's important to plan for the things you can't predict. You have to have flexibility, and you have to accept that there will be some volatility. You can't predict everything.

So how do you plan for what you can't predict? You'll drive yourself crazy if you try to imagine every possible scenario, but you can go into your planning with a mindset of flexibility.

In the last decade, there has been some real volatility in the market. You've likely seen those ups and downs affect many of your friends and colleagues. People who have tied their plans to a specific state of the economy can be thrown off track by any extra expense. Many people nearing retirement have now begun to account for market fluctuation; they've seen the damage that an economic downturn can cause.

And yet, when things become difficult for people in retirement, it's rarely because of any single factor. Usually stress is caused by a combination of choices made in retirement *and* circumstances that have arisen long beforehand. Whether it's due to a single bad decision or a variety of factors beyond one's control, people suffer when they fail to plan for change.

Many people struggle due to the economy, but there are also folks who have a hard time as the result of a personal or job situation. Wherever this kind of stress comes from, it can take over one's life.

JACQUELINE AND PETER'S STORY: SWIMMING THROUGH STRESS

For Jacqueline and Pete, economic factors combined with personal circumstances to create a perfect storm of **stress**. Though they worked hard and saved well, things simply didn't go their way. For thirty years, Jacqueline worked in the shipping department of a large corporation. By the time she was sixty, she was working in an office as a manager. But then something unexpected happened: her company was bought out. At first she was worried that she would lose her job entirely, but as it turned out, she ended up merely getting demoted back to the warehouse floor. She was a hard worker and dedicated to the company, but she just couldn't keep up. She was always making light of it, joking about her age and all, but she was worried. The truth was, Jacqueline didn't know how much longer she could continue working in that position before her body wouldn't take it any more.

Meanwhile, Jacqueline's husband Peter was struggling in his career. He was a self-employed electrician who worked all over the tri-county area, partnering with independent contractors on home construction and renovation. When times were good, he made a killing; he was the go-to guy for small-scale builds. But when the housing market took a dive, his work dried up. At the same time, Peter's colleagues in union jobs took pay cuts, but they kept their jobs. His situation was much less secure. For Peter, that situation was disastrous. He and Jacqueline had to liquidate some of their assets just to stay afloat.

Peter was concerned that they would end up having to take on debt just as they were on the cusp of retirement, but Jacqueline was firm in her insistence that they avoid owing money to a bank or other entity. They'd paid off their mortgage years earlier, long before it was due. Perhaps they'd been too aggressive in that area and neglected to account for the possibility of a rainy day. They were good savers, with good financial sense overall, but they found themselves without much of a cushion.

At that point, due to the economy, Peter and Jacqueline were in a state of *frustration*. They had a little room in their monthly budget and were still contributing to their retirement, but they were nervous about any problems arising. Even the smallest things could throw their budget for a loop. They didn't want to celebrate their achievements. When their friends would ask what they were planning to do for a birthday or anniversary, they would say, "We're just going to stay in; we can't afford to spend money." It was hard for others to watch them go through that, knowing that they would face even more strain when they were no longer able to work.

When the housing market picked back up and Peter's business was just barely going again, he fell and got injured on the job. Because of his injuries, he was forced to retire five years before he'd planned to do so. As an independent contractor, he had no company support when it came to disability. Peter took a hit in his annual income and had to start drawing his Social Security early.

At that point, Jacqueline was still working, but her mobility issues weren't getting any better. With Peter's injury, however, she had no choice. The company she worked for had no sympathy. Even though she'd been there for more than three decades—longer than most of the senior management—they only viewed her in terms of her profitability.

She tried to negotiate her unused sick days and vacation time to move up her retirement date, but the company refused. Jacqueline was deeply hurt by this; it was as if the company was telling her, over and over again, that she was expendable.

By the time she retired at sixty-five, Jacqueline felt bitter toward the company. She was barely able to save any additional money, and both her and Peter's health expenses kept rising.

Even though they had avoided debt and kept on top of their expenses, Jacqueline and Peter ended up in a state of **stress**. Now they have no flexibility in their budget. Any extra expense sends them into a paroxysm of worry. Their neighbors invite them over for dinner whenever they can, though Jacqueline and Peter always refuse any other offers of help. In the winter, their house is cold—just barely warm enough to keep the pipes from freezing.

Jacqueline and Peter don't complain about their situation, but their friends and neighbors can see their suffering. They're frustrated because they can't help out their siblings or treat their great-nephews or -nieces. If they have to pay up front for a prescription, they fly into a panic. Just imagine the toll all that anxiety takes on a person.

If you are full of stress and barely scraping by, there's very little you can do—and for Jacqueline and Peter, there's not much they could've done.

GEORGE'S STORY:
FROM FRUSTRATION TO TRIUMPH

George's life has been blessed, but it's never been easy. As he approached retirement, there were plenty of other challenges to overcome. He'd always been a successful scrap-steel trader, proud of his company and eager to do whatever it took to make it successful. As part of his work, he traveled all around the world. He was married, and he liked to treat his wife; when he went on trips, he would sometimes bring her along. To people on the outside, it appeared that George had the flexibility to take on whatever obstacles came his way.

The problem was that George may have been a little bit *too* comfortable. He worked hard, but he also thought that his good fortune would continue indefinitely. George had a pension through his company, but he never invested any money. Because his company promised to provide for him, George felt secure.

Unfortunately, things didn't go as planned. When George was forty-five, just as his daughter was beginning college, the steel company where he worked went bankrupt—the board's finance chair had been colluding with the CEO to make risky investments with money they'd embezzled from the company's pension funds. No one had had any idea what was happening. By the time the CFO found out, the money was gone.

Usually, pension funds are the first to be paid out in bankruptcy proceedings, but the steel trading company's attorneys argued that they should be able to liquidate the remaining pension funds completely in order to pay off outstanding debts. The Pension Benefit Guaranty Corporation, a government agency, had to step in to help the employees. In the end, they saved only 50 percent of the pensions' promised value. Many employees who had already retired faced huge life changes. In that sense, George was lucky: he got a new job and set up additional savings to offset what he'd lost.

Not long after the pension fiasco, George's daughter, Tricia, got into an accident and totaled her car. It wasn't her fault, but the insurance still didn't cover the full cost of a comparable replacement car. His daughter was still in college; she needed a car to get to school and work. With tuition payments to make, George ended up taking out a small personal loan to help Tricia, just until she could pay him back. It was a wake-up call for George. If he couldn't handle this problem without taking on debt, what would he do if something worse happened?

George was determined to be there for his loved ones, and he used that determination to motivate himself in his planning. He wanted to be sure he took every possible opportunity to prepare himself. He'd seen others who were full of regret because they'd had a chance to prepare themselves and didn't take it.

If you experience a loss like that, you look at things differently. You might wish someone had told you that your company's promises don't guarantee anything. The economy changes. Companies' profits rise and fall. People make mistakes.

Even just in the last decade, there have been major changes in the way people think about retirement. Pensions lose value; stocks lose steam. Those kinds of losses can happen to anyone. When you're planning for retirement, you have to account for those fluctuations if you're going to find *security* and *triumph*.

As George neared retirement, he was still trying to control everything in his budget, and this allowed him minimal room to grow. But as he approached the end of his career, he went through a drastic change that kept him from living according to his plan.

Due to circumstances that arose just prior to his retirement, George had a tough time for a while. He sank from a modicum of *security* down to *frustration*, but, eventually, he was able to turn his difficulties into *triumph*.

It's a sad story in some ways. When he was in his fifties, George's wife had an affair. Unbeknownst to him, she'd been draining their portfolio to pay for vacations with her boyfriend. When George thought his wife was going away to conferences for her job as a regional sales representative, she was actually jetting off to expensive resorts.

As soon as he discovered his wife's betrayal, George initiated divorce proceedings. He thought that he would be able to walk away in decent shape financially, but it turned out to be a difficult fight. He ended up being responsible for their mortgage, something he'd never planned to pay on his own. He now worked as a teacher—a job he loved—but he didn't make a lot of money. In this *frustration*, he began to come to terms with the fact that he didn't know how long it would take him to save enough to retire.

George's daughter was smart and self-sufficient; after she graduated from college, she went straight for her master's degree in education. As soon as she got a job as a math teacher, she started helping her father. George was about sixty then, and he'd just finished paying off his house. Once Tricia was helping with the property taxes, George was able to save a little more money. He didn't have much, but at age sixty-seven, he was finally able to retire.

George was living on a tight budget, but he didn't need a whole lot. He just wanted to be near his daughter. By this time, Tricia had married a police officer, and they had two young kids. They lived half a mile or so from George, so he spent a lot of time helping out his daughter.

But then, a few years later, Tricia's husband had a major heart attack while running a half marathon. He survived—barely—and while he went through surgery and rehab, George was there to help Tricia with the kids.

Then, due to a medical complication, Tricia's husband suddenly passed away.

Tricia plunged into profound grief. Her dreams were shattered. George wanted to do everything he could for his daughter. He couldn't help with the mortgage, but he could take care of the kids.

By the time Tricia returned to work, George had assumed primary parenting responsibilities. He was taking the kids to school, cooking, and doing the grocery shopping. He was even babysitting for other families from time to time to bring in extra money. All the while, he was squirreling away whatever he could for his grandkids. Whatever happened, he wanted to make sure they were taken care of. He worked hard to keep them safe and secure.

Then, George suddenly came down with pneumonia. He had always been active and healthy, but he'd grown weak in his later years. He passed away just after Christmas.

Tricia was devastated by the loss of her father, but she felt blessed by all that George had been able to do for them. Thanks to his careful planning, he'd left his grandchildren with healthy college funds. Though he hadn't been able to plan for everything, he'd insulated himself enough to help his family through a crisis. His sacrifice became their success.

Though things didn't work out seamlessly for George, he put his family first and ended up finding a sense of ease through whatever struggles arose. George began to see the obstacles more like speed bumps. His financial planning allowed him to approach each bump in the road with a sense of clarity and purpose. While he was shocked and saddened by the events that occurred in his life, he maintained a flexible outlook, finding stability in his family and community. While the setbacks he faced were no small thing, he was able to leave a profound legacy of *triumph*.

Life's ups and downs will always be present and can't be fully accounted for or predicted. With the right mind-set and asset management, however, we can maneuver around obstacles with more ease than we otherwise might if we are careless or leave things to chance.

How do you feel about your preparedness for dealing with situations beyond your control? Do you seize up, unable to imagine the next steps? Or do you take a calm look at your options to find the best solution in a difficult situation? Using the scorecard below, rate yourself on your preparedness for insecurity.

PERSONAL SCORE CARD – *Eight Things I Wish I Knew Before I Retired*

	IDEAL	REAL		
Mindset		So Not Me	I'm Working Toward	You Know Me So Well
I have dealt with the reality of life, and I am leaving behind a legacy I am proud of.		☐	☐	☐

CHAPTER 6

THERE WILL BE ANOTHER PAYCHECK

MELANIE'S STORY: FROM FAMILY STRESS TO PERSONAL TRIUMPH

AT THE END OF YOUR CAREER, THERE ARE PLENTY of changes to consider, but perhaps none so dramatic as the shift in where you get your income. The end of your working life creates new challenges for your life and your livelihood—but rest assured, there *will* be another paycheck.

A paycheck is more than just money in the bank; it's also recognition of a job well done. Seeing that pay stub or direct-deposit notification is one of the many ways in which we derive a sense of satisfaction from our work. In retirement, it can be difficult to feel the same gratification, even though you're drawing from the funds you've saved up over all those years. It's simply a matter of shifting your mind-set as you move forward.

For Melanie, the CFO of a midsized corporation, retirement plans were always automatic. She set her contributions and did the research to make sure her portfolio allocations were on track, but she didn't think much more about it. She was always focused on her work and her kids, both of whom she adored.

After she reached age sixty-five, her colleagues started asking her, "When are you going to get out of here?"

Every time, she'd respond, "Oh, I'm just having too much fun! I don't know that I'm ready."

Financially, Melanie had been ready for years; she probably could have retired once her kids had finished college. But even with her kids grown and out of the house, Melanie still felt like a single mom, holding the household together as she had for so many years. She loved to have fun, but Melanie was hardwired for caution. For her, working meant an extra layer of security from bringing home a paycheck. She simply wasn't ready to shift from accumulation to distribution yet. Even with a well-stocked emergency fund and a clear sense of what she needed financially, it was scary for Melanie to imagine not bringing home a paycheck as she had always done.

Melanie's caution was informed by her upbringing and by her close relationship with her mother. When Melanie's mother, Delores, retired, she had a very hard time with the idea of abandoning her job. It caused a lot of **stress**. Delores was a child of the Depression; her family had nearly starved in the Dust Bowl. It was impossible for her to willingly turn down a paycheck. Her generation dealt with a lot of insecurity early in life. Once Delores got to a place where things felt comfortable, it was hard for her to give that up.

All her life, Delores had been grateful just to have a job. After her family's early struggles, she'd started working as soon as she could, at age fourteen. She never went to college or trade school, and she didn't have any specialized training, so she always felt lucky to have a steady job on the assembly line at a packing plant. It was tough, physical work, and Melanie was relieved when her mother finally got promoted to personnel manager, a role she held for the next fifteen years of her career. Delores got to work in an office, off her feet. Melanie was much happier when her mother was writing schedules and managing budgets rather than wearing her body down with heavy lifting.

Unfortunately, her office position didn't last. When Delores was sixty-three, the company she worked for went through a crisis. Imported meat flooded the market, under-cutting domestic products. The company that Delores worked for was forced to restructure in order to survive in this new environment. They ended up slashing jobs in middle management to stay afloat. For Delores, that meant a return to the factory floor.

Delores never would have said so, but it was a disgrace. It's hard for older employees to get respect in such a physical workplace, never mind the pressure of keeping up with young and able-bodied people. At that point, Delores had back problems already, and the transition back to the assembly line only made those issues worse. Instead of spending weekend afternoons out at the baseball field watching her grandkids' Little League games, she had to rest at home. She wasn't one to complain, but she was having a very difficult time. But still, she refused to consider retiring.

"It's okay. I can take it," she always said.

Melanie knew her mother was tough. She didn't want to encroach on such a strong woman's independence, but she could see that her mother's job was affecting her well-being.

As a CFO, Melanie thought she might be able to use her professional skills to help her mother. She thought that demonstrating her mother's financial fitness for retirement might convince her that she was ready. So, with her mother by her side, Melanie went through the tedious process of manually calculating all of her mother's expenses and projected monthly income. She wanted her mother to see that she didn't have to keep doing that backbreaking work.

Melanie sat down with Delores and wrote out every single line item in her budget. Together, they constructed a balance sheet that showed what she needed and what her income would be, given her savings. Based on that analysis, it was clear that there was enough for her to retire comfortably, with plenty of cushion in case something unexpected occurred. But as much confidence as Delores had in her daughter's professional abilities, she didn't trust that she would actually have an income once she stopped working. She was a good saver and had a respectable nest egg, and she also had a pension. Even with just her Social Security benefits, she could've brought home nearly the same amount each month that she did from working. But it was like Delores had a mental block and couldn't accept Melanie's forecast for a rosy retirement.

Melanie's father had passed away a few years earlier. Delores had been collecting his Social Security, but she wasn't spending it; she was depositing it straight into her savings! With that additional income, she had accumulated more than $180,000 on top of her emergency fund. Yet she wouldn't budge.

For nine years, Melanie tried to show her mother that she could make it. Melanie wanted her to be able to stop worrying so much and enjoy all that she'd worked for. But it was never enough—no matter how Melanie laid it out, her mother couldn't connect the dots.

She'd say, "Oh, maybe I'll retire next year," but she never did.

Delores had all the resources she needed to stop working. She simply lacked the confidence to leave her job. She worked until she was seventy-two; she didn't stop until she got sick and could no longer make it to work. After a quick decline, she passed away.

This inability to visualize how she would get paid in retirement created a situation of **stress** for Delores. She was accustomed to going to work every day and having a paycheck deposited into her account every two weeks. She knew exactly what she had to do at work in order to earn her pay, and she knew she would earn a bonus at the end of the year if she'd done an outstanding job. She simply couldn't get over her anxiety about transitioning into a totally different structure of earnings.

Although Melanie did the best she could, she still feels like she should have done more to get her mother to stop working toward the end of her career. When she encountered family and friends in the same situation, Melanie tried to help them understand that there *would* be another paycheck in retirement.

Melanie worried that her brother would never retire. He loved to work; his job was an extension of who he was as a person. When Melanie and her brother were kids, he was always finding new ways to fix things. She remembers him repairing a broken radio with an old bike spoke! He studied statistics and became an analyst for a big security firm while his wife worked part-time as a nurse at a pediatrician's office. Melanie's brother was brilliant with corporate strategic analysis, but he never quite trusted himself when it came to his own portfolio. It can be hard to take your own advice.

Melanie's brother knew, intellectually, that he was doing the right things to enable him and his wife, Sarah Beth, to retire, but things kept coming up in his life that made him nervous. Sarah Beth's brother had struggled with alcoholism over the years, and he had always supported his wife in stepping in to help their family when things got really bad.

Whenever Melanie tried to broach the subject of retirement with her brother, he said, "I'll just keep working until I'm seventy. I'll get a bigger Social Security check and I'll be sure that my family is taken care of." He seemed to be at peace with that solution.

Melanie's sister-in-law, on the other hand, was having a hard time. She, too, was still working, and was much less satisfied in her career than her husband was. Although she believed in her work as a pediatric nurse, she was very frustrated with her working environment. Sarah Beth had been at the practice longer than any of the other nurses, and she was training many of the new arrivals, but she wasn't getting paid for her expertise. Around her sixtieth birthday, a new doctor became the head of the practice and instituted a pay cap for all non-physician staff, leaving her stuck at her current salary, without the possibility of another raise. Even though she loved her work, she felt demoralized when she was left with no possibility for advancement. The lack of respect and recognition was hard for her to handle. Melanie could understand; it was a terrible situation to be put in.

Then, when Sarah Beth was sixty-four and her brother was sixty-nine, Sarah Beth was diagnosed with Hodgkin's disease, a type of cancer. Fortunately, Hodgkin's disease has a very low mortality rate, and after one round of chemo, Sarah Beth was cancer-free.

She was all ready to get back to work when, all of a sudden, she lost all feeling in her hands. She was suffering from a condition known as peripheral neuropathy, an occasional side effect of chemotherapy. Usually, peripheral neuropathy goes away after a few months, but for Sarah Beth, that didn't happen. Her husband was determined to get her the best care possible to help her regain the use of her hands. They went to the best neurologists available, but because the insurance company classified her treatment as "nonessential," they would only cover 50 percent of the cost.

It cost about $40,000 to get the treatments that ultimately restored Sarah Beth's motor skills, and she and Melanie's brother ended up having to pay $20,000 of that.

This expense required them to dip into their 401(k). At that point, Melanie's brother told her, "I can't retire until I'm seventy because I need my Social Security check to be larger." He was perfectly willing to work until he was seventy, but Melanie didn't want that for her brother. She could see that he was in a state of real *frustration*, and she considered trying to use her skills to help her brother manage his finances. But after what had happened with their mother, Melanie was wary of getting intimately involved with her brother's finances. After her experience struggling against her mother's mental impasse, she decided to help her brother seek out his own information. She gave him the resources he needed, and he got to work—and by then, he was motivated.

Throughout his career, Melanie's brother had focused primarily on building his 401(k), and he'd neglected to take Social Security into account. When he started looking into the information Melanie had given him, he realized he'd been operating under faulty assumptions. He hadn't known what his options were.

The next time he talked to his sister, he was tickled pink. Normally a steady, matter-of-fact type of person, he was giddy to the point of laughing out loud because he'd just found out that he would be getting an extra $1,200 in Social Security benefits each month. That deposit was his first retirement paycheck.

Once he realized that he had benefits that he hadn't known about before, he decided to keep looking into the income sources he would have in his retirement. Because he worked for a big security firm, he had a pension plan in addition to his investments. He realized, though, that he hadn't taken a look at that plan in a very, very long time. His information was woefully out of date. Because his company had been acquired by another corporation, he wasn't entirely clear on the benefits that were available to him.

As it turned out, there was an excellent pension plan at the original company where he'd worked. Even after it was bought out, the pension plan was still in place. In fact, Melanie's brother was supposed to begin receiving payouts from that original plan when he turned sixty-five. He'd had no idea; when he finally reached that plan's provider, he found out that they'd tried to contact him, but they'd had the wrong information. He was supposed to receive about $3,500 each month.

Because Melanie's brother was already sixty-eight by the time he found out about the pension, the fund immediately sent him a check for $125,000. It was quite a surprise! Melanie's brother was a high earner, but a lump sum like that was unprecedented. When he and his wife sat down together to talk about how to manage their windfall, they took a look at all the sources of income that they'd be receiving, and they saw that they'd be earning more in retirement than when they were working. This was certainly welcome news; they could hardly believe it.

"I don't know how we're going to spend all this money!" he told Melanie. Instead of having to wait until age seventy, Melanie's brother got to retire at age sixty-eight. He now gets to spend much more time with his grandkids, and his wife was able to leave her unsatisfying job. She still works as a nurse, though—volunteering part-time at a free clinic.

After many decades of hard work, Melanie's brother and sister-in-law have reached a state of *security* that they couldn't have dreamed of before. They know where their income comes from, and they're more than comfortable with the amount they receive. Even so, they watch their accounts closely; it's just how they're accustomed to living.

Melanie's outlook on her own retirement has been formed by the long process of watching her brother and sister-in-law reach their own *security*. Because she still enjoys her work and the mental stimulation it provides, she isn't in a rush to retire. But she knows that when she does, she wants to live in a way that doesn't require her to be constantly reviewing her accounts and managing her money.

When Melanie began her career, she worked in outside sales for a chemical manufacturer. Very quickly, the company recognized that she was a gifted financial analyst—through her manipulations of order quantity and shipping costs, she was able to net far greater returns than her colleagues. She rose through the company's ranks, reaching her position as CFO by age forty. As the first woman and the youngest person at the company to hold that position, she felt gratified by the trust the board had placed in her.

At the same time, Melanie continued to feel anxious about her personal finances. Because she'd gotten divorced in her early thirties, she had to navigate a complicated web of legal entanglements, custody, and childcare. As a result, when her children were young, she lived more or less paycheck to paycheck. Her children never went without things they needed, but they learned not to lust after the next new thing.

Melanie's off-the-wall sense of humor helped her get through those years when she often lost sleep over the regular bills. She would leave work, pick up her kids, and make dinner with jokes at the ready. Melanie was always playing around with her kids, who adored their mother for her kindness and dependable positive attitude. They always knew she would put them first.

While Melanie was still advancing in her career, any extra expense really threw her for a loop. For example, when her daughter Julia was in sixth grade, she won the local science fair, advancing to the state level. Melanie was thrilled for her daughter's accomplishment, but at the same time, she was barely making ends meet. She ended up having to ask her brother for help to pay for the hotel room at the state competition. He was happy to help, of course, but her pride took a real hit when she made that call.

Yet, even when things were at their toughest, Melanie put money away for her children's college funds *and* contributed the maximum matching amount to her own retirement. Even if it meant that she and the kids would eat hot dogs and spaghetti for dinner, she knew that it was crucial to invest in their future.

When Melanie's career advancement caught up with her abilities, she became more comfortable with the ebb and flow of her monthly expenses. By the time her kids were in high school, she was breathing a little easier.

Still, the looming prospect of college tuition weighed on Melanie. She knew that her ex-husband had little to contribute. Though she had been contributing to her kids' college funds since they were born, she simply couldn't keep up with the exponential pace of tuition increases. At the same time, Melanie didn't want to hold back her children's potential. She wanted her son and daughter to be able to attend the best colleges they were able to earn their way into.

When it came time for her daughter, Julia, to apply to college, Melanie insisted that she apply only to the best programs in her field. She'd distinguished herself in science and math throughout her schooling, and she had a chance to attend a top program. Julia was determined to make a career in astrophysics, a notoriously difficult discipline, and Melanie was dedicated to supporting her daughter's entry into that challenging field. Melanie swore to Julia that she would find the money to send her wherever she gained admittance.

When Julia decided to attend an astronomy and technology program, she knew that her financial aid package would only cover half of her cost of attendance. Julia offered to take out student loans in her own name, but her mother wouldn't hear of it.

"I can't let you start out in debt," she told her daughter. Melanie decided that *she* would take out the student loans instead.

Melanie's financial advisor cautioned her against that decision, but it was of no use; she was dead set on it. She was taking a big risk by assuming more than $50,000 in debt at age forty-six, but she wanted to do everything in her power to help her daughter succeed.

At that point, Melanie had earned her position as CFO, but she wasn't making as much money as many men in the same position in the same field. Using her strong people skills and financial acumen, Melanie convinced the company's board of directors that she deserved a 20 percent raise. Because she'd been so successful—and because she agreed to sign a ten-year contract with a non-compete clause—Melanie got her raise and was able to pay off the debt from her daughter's education in just five years.

Melanie's sense of humor has helped her to remain flexible. She hasn't let go of her meticulous eye for detail, but as she considers her retirement, she *has* begun to look for ways to spend less time thinking about her money. At age seventy-two, Melanie is still working, but only by choice. She wants to save enough so that she can take home the same annual income she does now, without touching her emergency fund. Even though she's great at balancing a budget, she doesn't want to worry about that in her retirement; she's planning to focus on the long-term of her financial life, rather than the day-to-day.

In some ways, Melanie's experiences in her working life have shaped the *triumph* of her outlook in retirement. Her years of living paycheck to paycheck taught her to plan ahead and prepare. In allocating her income distributions, she's given her expenses room to grow, and the market, room to shrink. Given Melanie's history, she's sure to make it happen.

Finding *triumph* in retirement means having the confidence that those paychecks will be there, providing for what you need and leading to the higher purpose to which you devote your life. It's crucial to keep in mind the bigger impact you want to make, then work backward to figure out how to get there. Melanie's success comes from that clarity, and from her determination. It's not about how much money she has; it's about knowing that she doesn't have to think about her future.

The idea of leaving behind the security of a regular paycheck can be truly daunting. It keeps folks like Melanie's mother from ever retiring—an outcome we hate to witness. Everyone deserves to find happiness and fulfillment at the end of their working life.

The problem is, we're trained to think in terms of our paychecks. From the time you started working, you've probably arranged your household accounting around that kind of system.

In retirement, things will change. You may receive Social Security on one schedule while receiving disbursements from your pension and/or 401(k) on a different schedule. Whatever the arrangement of your income happens to be, the important thing is to understand where it's coming from and how much it will be. When you understand your income and expenses, and when you're able to let go of worrying about how you'll get paid, you can find **triumph.**

Using the scorecard below, rate yourself on your retirement paycheck.

8

PERSONAL SCORE CARD – *Eight Things I Wish I Knew Before I Retired*

Mindset	So Not Me	I'm Working Toward	You Know Me So Well
IDEAL	REAL		
My plan is working, and allows me to live a stress-free lifestyle with clarity and independence.	☐	☐	☐

CHAPTER 7

NO ONE GETS OUT ALIVE

Even after digging through the details of debt, disbursement, and purpose, there are still some retirement conversations no one wants to have. When it comes to the subject of legacy, almost everyone feels uncomfortable; it's simply difficult to think about what will happen after we die.

Many people experience anxiety about estate planning. It's hard to imagine how the world will view you when you're no longer around. Once you've passed on, your legacy will be out of your control. Only the actions you took while you were here will matter; there will be no way to change the conditions already in place.

Death isn't a pleasant topic of conversation, but the fact is, no one gets out of this world alive. Whether we like it or not, we all have to leave this life. Whatever you've done during your time on this earth will have to stand for you and your name. The question is: What do you want to leave behind?

If you don't start planning your estate while you're alive, you'll relinquish control of your legacy to the winds of fate. If you shy away from the discomfort of talking about death, you'll willingly give away your chance to leave an impact on future generations.

Many people are too frightened to look beyond retirement, toward what they'll leave behind. For the most part, however, they aren't necessarily afraid of death itself; they're afraid of dying and not having their lives mean something. They want their legacy to contribute to a higher purpose.

What do you want your life to mean once you're gone?

This question is similar to the question of purpose in retirement; it cuts to the heart of who you are and what values you hold. Those who have found *security* or *triumph* with their purpose often have an easier time identifying what they want their legacies to be. They have clarity.

However, estate planning tends to be quite different from planning for retirement. There are many more unknowns, and more variables for which to account. It's a different kind of strategic thinking. Sometimes people will come to us with an exact sum of money as a goal. They'll say, "I want to leave $25,000 behind." But with estate planning, it's difficult to pin down an exact sum that will be available at the end of someone's life. Who knows what will happen: Will you need expensive medical care? How will your assets be allocated at that point? How much will your net worth be?

Amid all the uncertainty, it's important to think about what's reasonable to expect and what can't be planned ahead of time. Everyone's ideal outcome is different. Some people like to fill in all the details; others like to leave the more particular decisions up to their loved ones. The most important thing is simply to have a plan in place.

DANIEL'S STORY:
A LEGACY OF STRESS

Daniel was a single man in his early sixties. After divorcing twenty years earlier, he lived simply, in a trailer with a wooden deck for leisure activities, and a work shed on his property for various projects. If anything broke, he fixed it himself, and he took care of maintaining his own land. He wasn't a big spender, and his finances were relatively organized.

Right around when Daniel was planning to retire, he was diagnosed with pancreatic cancer. This turn of events was devastating, of course, but because Daniel lived near a great hospital, at least he had access to good medical care. His cousin Judith, with whom he was close, lived nearby, and she helped him get to and from doctor's appointments when he needed an extra hand. Given the situation, things were going about as well as they could.

The problem was Daniel's two children. Daniel's relationship with his children had been strained since his divorce. Although they were grown and married with families of their own, they still relied on their father for money. They constantly called him up to guilt-trip him about their childhood and demand that he make payments on their car or their new stereo. He felt like he was partially responsible for their dysfunction, so he kept paying up, no matter how many times his cousin Judith counseled him to do otherwise.

Every time Judith tried to talk to Daniel about getting his will in order, he'd say, "I'll do it soon. But even if I don't, it won't be *my* mess to take care of."

Judith hated hearing him talk like that. She couldn't believe that he'd really want to leave his loved ones with unsettled property and accounts. And what if the state had to step in?

She used to tell him, "Our state can't even pass a budget! Do you really want to leave your legacy in its hands?"

But still, Daniel would just shake his head. In some ways, it's easy to understand why Daniel didn't feel motivated to arrange his estate. His stress in estate planning was partially due to the distance between him and his children; they constantly took advantage of him, and leaving them with a mess to sort through would be a kind of emotional retribution. Eventually, after much soul-searching and Judith's constant advice that it was the right thing to do, Daniel had an attorney draw up his will.

When Daniel's kids asked for money, Judith always told him, "You have to say no. They can do it on their own. They're going to have to learn at some point."

But Daniel kept sending them money.

When Daniel's cancer advanced to stage 4, he was no longer able to care for himself. Judith stepped in, doing all the things Daniel couldn't do for himself. All the while, Daniel's children kept calling to ask for money—but they never called to ask about their father's well-being.

Judith was deeply disturbed by the children's behavior, which she witnessed firsthand when Daniel became so sick that he had to move into her home. Judith didn't have much extra space, so she settled Daniel into the sleeper sofa in her living room. At least, there, he could enjoy watching the birds fly around the feeder on her deck.

By the time Daniel died, his kids hadn't seen him for years. They hadn't even come to visit their father on his deathbed. They didn't live far away; they simply didn't make the effort—that is, until their father was already gone. When Judith called the children to tell them their father had died, she was shocked by their responses. His son simply asked when the funeral was; his daughter asked if Judith could pay her way there. Neither one offered to help with their father's service.

Of course, everyone deals with grief in his or her own way. Judith tried to understand what Daniel's kids might be feeling, but when they showed up, she couldn't believe their behavior. Daniel had named Judith as the executor of his will, and the legal proceedings became very tense. As soon as they gathered together at Daniel's trailer to go through his things, his kids asked, "So, how much money is there?"

Sometimes there isn't an easy answer to that question. With taxes to take into account, there can be a few different ways to look at the sum of money that remains after someone has died. Judith recommended that they draw the funds over several years to minimize the taxes they had to pay. But the kids wouldn't hear of it; they wanted all the money, right away.

"What's the fastest way to get it?" his daughter asked. She didn't consider what her father would've wanted her to do, or what use of the money would do the most good for her and her family. She only wanted to get as much as she could, as quickly as possible.

Daniel's cousin Judith, who had cared for him in his last days, felt bereft. She felt stressed by this terrible situation.

The children were fighting over material things and not even thinking about their departed father. Their fraught relationship had turned into a worst-case scenario just for a legacy. In the end, Daniel's children didn't even consider their father's memory as they moved forward.

JIM AND CAMILA'S STORY: FROM FRUSTRATION TO TRIUMPH IN ONE GENERATION

Camila's situation was starkly different from Daniel's, but it shared one characteristic: hesitation. No one likes to think about estate planning. Many people leave old plans in place simply because they don't want to deal with the stress of creating new ones.

When Camila was in her fifties, she had a will, but it was old; she'd written it when her kids were young. After the scramble to get a guardianship document in place, it's very common for people to forget about any kind of estate planning. Once she made sure her children would be taken care of, Camila filed her documents away and didn't make a single change in them for more than forty years. It wasn't until tragedy struck her family that Camila began thinking about getting her affairs in order.

There are many reasons people fail to update their plans. Some people are simply too busy to take the time to schedule it. Others disagree with their spouse about what to do, and avoiding the subject is a way of skirting marital conflict. Often there's a psychological barrier that pops up when people think about estate planning. "If I start planning for my death," they think, "then surely I will die soon."

Many people experience mental roadblocks that keep them stuck in a state of *frustration*. They think about estate planning as something to do later, when the time is right. They think they need to wait until they finish paying off their mortgages, or until they're retired. They just keep putting it off, kicking it down the road until it's too late.

Perhaps part of the reason Camila delayed her estate planning was her husband, Jim. Jim was ten years older than Camila, and when he had to retire at seventy-one, they still had a lot of debt. They worked and worked to pay off about $85,000 in credit card, mortgage, and other debt. It took a *lot* for them to get through that, and Camila couldn't retire until they finally hoisted the anchor of a lifetime's worth of debt.

Jim and Camila were never big spenders, but they cut back on everything in order to escape their *frustration*. Jim used to go hunting in Wisconsin every year, but he ended those trips when he retired, and didn't go hunting again for the next ten years while Camila was still working. They did absolutely everything they could to relieve themselves of their debt.

As soon as they'd paid off the last of their debt, Camila quit the advertising agency where she'd worked for forty years. She was thrilled to finally be able to step away from her desk and find purpose outside of working long hours to serve her clients. They'd made it!

But then, just as they began to discuss revising their wills (which were forty years old at that point), Camila noticed that Jim was moving around more slowly. When they went for walks around their neighborhood, he easily became out of breath. He was more tired than he used to be. After a few months, she insisted that they visit the doctor—together.

The news wasn't good. The doctor told them that Jim's heart was in trouble; he'd been experiencing small, frequent heart attacks that just felt to Jim like moments of fatigue or anxiety. Because this series of heart attacks had gone unnoticed, his heart was terribly damaged.

According to the doctor, Jim had only one therapeutic option: open-heart surgery. At eighty-one years old, it was a big risk to take. But given the alternative, he was determined to give it a chance. They had to act quickly.

You never know when a health problem will suddenly consume your life; it can happen at any age. When it does, you want to be in a position to focus on getting the best possible care, not on logistical complications.

Camila wished that they had settled their estate plans sooner. While she could've been spending quality time with

Jim and their kids before her husband underwent major surgery, Camila was sifting through life insurance plans, pension benefits, and Social Security paperwork. She was bogged down with the details of designating beneficiaries and making sure all of their assets were listed in both of their names. Camila was frustrated to be dealing with all of this documentation at such a stressful time.

When it came time for the surgery, Jim and Camila's kids came into town. They'd planned to be there for the surgery, and then take turns staying with their parents to assist with Jim's recovery. Jim's estate plan was in place before he went into surgery, with his money directed to Judith in the event that he didn't survive. After fifty years of marriage, Jim knew that if he passed, Camila would ensure that his legacy was well taken care of.

During surgery, another tiny heart attack ruptured one of Jim's arteries. The doctors did everything they could for him, but he didn't make it. Camila was left reeling from the events of the past few months. She had just retired after working her way out from under all that debt, and now she was a widow. Things had changed so quickly.

After Jim died, Camila wanted to get her estate plans in order as soon as possible. "If I drop dead tomorrow, I want to know that my family will be taken care of," she said. Camila sat down with her daughter and her lawyer, whom she named as her executor. They listed all of her assets and all of her beneficiaries. They went through each asset, one by one, with the financial advisor, noting the specific uses and benefits of each type of holding in her portfolio. As it turned out, Camila and Jim had each recently inherited money from family members who had passed away. Not long after paying off her debt, Camila found herself with significant additional resources. She hadn't expected to end up with any extra money; it was a huge surprise to her. It presented additional options and questions for the estate process, but ultimately those were happy decisions to make.

While keeping her emergency fund and monthly disbursements intact, Camila, her daughter, and her lawyer parsed out each of the items so that nothing would be left to chance. She set up trusts for her beneficiaries, deciding to set money aside for her church as well as her family.

Some people want to leave trusts to foundations, religious organizations, or educational institutions. Some want their families to get their money. Whatever your goals, you have to plan ahead. By establishing clear guidance, Camila ensured that her legacy reached a place of *security*.

At that point, Camila was able to relax a little. Rather than waiting until the last minute, as her husband had, she'd gathered the resources she had and made sure she knew where they were going. Once trusts were in place, and once that stability had cemented her legacy, Camila would be leaving her family and community better off than they were before. That was her only goal.

Sometimes, when people inherit money, they have a hard time coping with a new resource that becomes available amid their grief over a lost loved one. They don't know what to do with the money; they feel guilty about spending it. Would their uncle be supportive of them using the money to pay down a debt, or would he rather they use it for a vacation? What use of an inheritance will best honor a lost loved one?

In those situations, it helps to have a strong relationship with the person who has passed on. The beneficiary can look back on their time with the deceased and consider that person's values. How would that person *really* want the money to be spent? How would they want their beneficiaries to use the fruits of their life's labor?

With legacy, **triumph** comes when you're able to pass down not just money to the next generation, but also values. When Camila set up those trusts for her children, she instilled in them the importance of looking out for the future. While some people designate the exact percentages of their estate to be allotted to each grandchild and other relatives, Camila left those details up to her children. She simply wanted them to know that they were taken care of.

Camila passed away ten years or so after her husband, Jim, and her children inherited their trusts. They went straight to the financial advisor their mother had consulted. They wanted to make sure they were managing their money responsibly so that they could one day leave legacies of their own. Those values had become multigenerational.

Today, Camila's two children talk much more openly about their estate plans than their parents did. Even though they're only in their fifties, they're conscientious about updating their wills every five years or so, or whenever their portfolios or family situations change. They know that death can come at any time, and they want their families to feel blessed, not burdened, by their legacies.

Camila learned to take estate planning and death seriously. From her life experiences, she saw that death was no different from retirement. You can't predict the exact moment when it will happen until it gets very close, but you have to plan far ahead of time in order for it to go smoothly.

Even though Camila passed away more than ten years ago, her children still beam when they talk about her. She wasn't just a wonderful grandmother, mother, and wife; she was also a resourceful planner. Because of her example, her children believe in putting in the planning and preparation on the front end to make sure everything works out the way they want it to. When people ask how they got their money, they're candid about it. They say, "My parents earned it."

When people inherit money from someone they love and respect, they're much more likely to save it and use it for a higher purpose. By spending their inheritance responsibly, and by continuing to talk about what their parents would have wanted, Camila and Jim's children honor their parents' legacies.

Legacy isn't just money; it's a responsibility that's passed down. After you die, the relationships you built will guide the loved ones you've left behind. As you've seen here, legacy is much more than a trust or a check.

Of course, not everyone can leave behind a significant sum of money, but if you don't create solid estate plans for those charged with carrying out your last wishes, you'll be remembered for leaving a mess. As you plan your retirement, it's also important to consider what comes after, and how your mind-set during your retirement will play into how you shape your legacy.

Think about your assets, your responsibilities, and the legacy you want to leave. When was the last time you updated your estate plans? Do you feel comfortable with the plans you have in place?

Using the scorecard below, rate yourself on your estate planning and preparedness.

---

⑧ PERSONAL SCORE CARD – *Eight Things I Wish I Knew Before I Retired*

	IDEAL	REAL		
Mindset		So Not Me	I'm Working Toward	You Know Me So Well
Being debt-free allows me to live confidently in a world that is ever changing.		☐	☐	☐

CHAPTER 8

MIND-SET FOR THE FUTURE: IT'S GOING TO BE ALL RIGHT

As YOU'VE MADE YOUR WAY THROUGH THIS BOOK, you've acquired plenty of tools to help you succeed in retirement. But along with the wisdom these stories have conveyed, they may have planted some feelings of insecurity or doubt.

Right now, you may be feeling unsure of yourself. You may be asking yourself, "Have I done everything I could have done to succeed? What if I could've done more?"

It may have felt daunting to read through the *Eight Things I Wish I Knew*, score yourself on each one, and consider ways you could improve, but retirement isn't just about preparedness; it's also about having a positive mind-set.

Whether you believe you can or you believe you can't, you're right. If you believe that you're at the mercy of the markets, the political situation, or the obstacles that your family might face, then you will be. But if you're confident in yourself and mentally prepared to take on whatever comes, *everything is going to be OK.*

Often the anticipation of an event is far worse than the event itself. It's easy to imagine the worst that can happen, thinking through all the catastrophes that might befall you. You may compare yourself to other people—their vacations, cars, and home renovations; it's easy to imagine that other people's lives are more glamorous than our own. But at the end of the day, life is not about leaving behind millions of dollars or a big house. It's about the memories we leave for others.

If you worry about retirement, or about anything in life, what does that worry do? It revs up your anxiety, which is detrimental to your health. But it doesn't make anything better. You can't change the past, or take back any mistakes you made, but you *can* decide your future. When you build your purpose and identity in retirement, you create a positive turn toward the future. You stop saying, "I'm a factory worker," and start saying, "I'm a great-grandfather," or "I'm a woodworker," or "I'm a deacon." Your identity should help you to keep moving. Whatever your forward-thinking purpose in life, focus on how it can be productive.

Of course, in retirement and aging, things are going to go wrong. When they do, the important thing is to have a sense of humor. The people who have the most fun in their old age are the ones who joke about it.

Imagine a man in his seventies who has been bald for twenty years. When another bald man walks into the room, he'll say, "Great haircut!" Around other bald people, he seeks out that bond, that connection. He uses humor as a way to connect with people, and it puts everyone at ease.

When you're dealing with a taboo topic, stating the obvious releases the tension. Whether it's your hair, your age, or another kind of insecurity, you can use humor as a way to cope. Let the posturing and the barriers come down. What do you have to lose?

When it's all over, if you're around the people who love you and you're feeling taken care of, you'll be in a great place. We want you to know that your best is good enough. You'll get through it all and end up with everything you need to succeed.

Mind-set is a difficult thing to quantify or place on a continuum, but these stories will show you that, even when you're struggling, you can still find a way to feel successful. Your retirement will be what you make of it. Here we'll share two stories to show you how you can take control of your attitude and reach a position of *triumph*.

HERBERT AND BECKY'S STORY: MAKING THE MOST OF WHATEVER YOU HAVE

There's no way to avoid some struggles, but Herbert is determined to face whatever obstacles come his way with dignity and grace.

"I live in the United States of America, the greatest country in the world," he says proudly. "I have my friends here, and I have my home. While I still have my health, everything else is secondary."

The sources of Herbert's stress are sometimes personal and sometimes financial; the two are almost always intertwined. Herbert was married for more than forty years. He and his wife, Becky, had a daughter, Aimee, whom they raised on their parcel of homestead land in northern Wisconsin. They lived off the land as much as possible. Becky raised chickens and kept a few dairy cows in addition to horses they used to harvest timber. At the same time, Herbert was also a union ironworker. True, theirs was a one-horse town with few diversions, but they were rooted in their tight-knit community. Becky and Herbert were very happy there.

Their restless daughter, however, wasn't as happy in the small town she was raised in. Growing up, she was always running off and getting in trouble with boys. On more than one occasion she ran away to the city for the weekend, sending Herbert and Becky into a panic. When Aimee disappeared like that, Becky wouldn't leave the house; she'd sit by the phone smoking like a chimney as she waited for a call. Herbert, however, would calmly take his keys and go looking for his daughter.

Through all that strife, Herbert and Becky did everything they could for Aimee. The first action they took was to send her to a military boarding school. Herbert was a traditional man, and he thought that discipline and structure were the only ways to get Aimee in line. The academy was expensive; Herbert and Becky had to dip into their 401(k) in order to afford it and Becky took another job. They didn't think twice about it though. They were confident that their daughter's education, and getting help for her behavioral problems, would be worth the steep price.

Unfortunately, it didn't work out that way. Aimee ran away from the military academy so many times that she was expelled. After that, they found a therapeutic boarding school offering education and therapy for youths with behavioral disorders and learning disabilities. They worked with social workers and other kinds of professionals to get their daughter help. Every time she ran away, they turned to private investigators and social services to bring her home.

All the while, Herbert and Becky were still rooted in their community. They helped their neighbors to cure wood and raise barns; they tended their livestock and gardens. Although Becky was working full-time, she kept expanding her garden, even building a farm stand out by their mailbox so their neighbors could buy their extra vegetables and eggs. If you went by their house on any given day, Becky might tell you, "Oh, I've just ripped down the old toolshed and built a new chicken coop from the scrap wood." The farm was part of who they were.

Because of their daughter's continually escalating needs, Herbert and Becky kept having to forego saving money to pay for her treatment. They never questioned that sacrifice. They did what they thought was right. Aimee was able to stay put for a couple of years at the second therapeutic boarding school where her parents sent her. Her grades were halfway decent for the first time in her life, and her therapist believed that she was making real strides in confronting her anger issues. She even started taking on weekend work shifts at the school's carpentry shop. Having grown up on her parents' homestead, she had the basic skills already. But then, in April of her senior year of high school, just weeks after turning eighteen, she disappeared without a trace.

This came as quite a shock to Becky and Herbert. They'd thought their daughter was making great strides, so they were absolutely blindsided.

Because Aimee was eighteen, legally an adult, Herbert and Becky had fewer options for pursuing her. What's more, this disappearance was different from the earlier ones: she'd left her cell phone at school, so they couldn't track her through its signal. From information they gathered later, it seemed that she'd been stealing money from her classmates since she'd arrived at the boarding school. She'd likely escaped with more than a thousand dollars in cash.

For all their years of marriage, Becky and Herbert had firmly maintained a united front when dealing with Aimee's troubles. But now they couldn't agree on a course of action. Becky wanted to let her go, to stop looking and wait for her to come back home on her own. She wanted to put ads in the papers of the major cities nearby, but otherwise, she didn't believe that chasing after Aimee was the solution. And once Aimee was found, Becky doubted she could be forced to stay.

Herbert, on the other hand, was willing to stop at nothing to find his baby girl. He worried that she wouldn't have a safe place to live, and that she was in serious physical danger. What if she was living on the street? What if she got sick or injured and couldn't get help in time?

Over the next year, Herbert and Becky couldn't reach any semblance of a truce. Both were dead set in their opinions, sure they were right. While Herbert drained his paychecks and accumulated debt to pay for private investigators, Becky fumed and worked in her garden. At the end of that year, Becky told Herbert to leave; she was filing for divorce.

Herbert, to his credit, did as his wife asked. He left her with the house, which was already paid off, and had to buy a place of his own—not an easy thing to do with the significant credit card debt he'd accumulated. He had to take a higher interest rate than he otherwise would have, which drained even more from his paychecks.

At this point, Herbert was more than $75,000 in debt. He couldn't keep paying private investigators. He was devastated to have lost his daughter, and now his wife, but he still kept looking toward the future. While his colleagues, also in their late fifties, were declining overtime shifts, he started taking on as many as he could. He worked late hours, pushed his body to the absolute limit, and always came home exhausted.

Still, Herbert didn't complain. Sometimes he would look at his checking account and think, *I wish I'd done things differently*, but he didn't let that thought linger for too long. He kept moving forward.

Divorce was Herbert's financial wake-up call. He realized that he couldn't keep spending tens of thousands of dollars to search for his daughter; he had to take care of himself first. He saw his friends enjoying time with their families, taking their grandchildren out on the boat and teaching them how to fish. He sometimes felt a little resentment. He saw what he didn't have. It's a natural feeling; he was grieving over his profound losses.

But at the same time, Herbert kept looking to the future. No matter what the situation, he tried to find a positive aspect of it. When he had to move out of the farm homestead he loved and find a new place to live, he knew he'd have to downsize significantly. He decided to look for a home in an area close to a community garden, where he could still plant his own seeds and grow his own food, even though he had to live in a very small house with no arable land. When the weather was nice enough, and he wasn't picking up extra shifts, he was out in the garden. He just loved being outside and working the land.

Herbert didn't forget about his daughter, but he tried to keep himself from collapsing into a state of panic like he had the first year she was gone. For the next ten years he worked and worked, paying down his debt and trying to make the best of his situation.

Then, one day, he got a call from Becky. Although their marriage had collapsed, they were still on speaking terms; they lived in the same small town and attended the same church. She wasn't in a great state financially, either, but she'd inherited some money from a relative who had died, so she was experiencing less frustration than Herbert.

It was their daughter, Becky said. "She called me. She's in Chicago. She wants to come see us."

Herbert couldn't believe it. Neither of them had heard from her in all those years; he was sure that she was either dead or lost forever.

As it turned out, their daughter had had a few close brushes with death over the years since her disappearance. After she ran away from school, she'd left the country, moving to a small island in the South Pacific. She'd become involved with drugs and unsavory characters, seeking all kinds of dangerous escapes from her feelings. But eight years after her disappearance, while she was still on the island, she'd met an American soldier who was on leave. She and the soldier became friends and kept in touch after he went back to his base in Japan. They wrote to each other, communicated via video chat, and cultivated a deep sense of trust. Over time, their relationship grew.

Now, two years later, their daughter had finally come back to the United States—as an Army wife. She had called her mother to begin the process of reuniting with her family.

Becky and Herbert met their daughter and her husband a few weeks later. The meeting was fraught. At times it was tearful; at times, awkward; at times, cathartic. But it was a turning point. These days, things still aren't perfect, but Herbert feels blessed to have his daughter back in his life. He's overjoyed that she is now expecting her first child; he can't wait to be a grandfather.

Herbert has lost a lot, but he's found a way to live with what he has left. He does contract-based ironworking, so he's able to take a little time off when he has to. He knows he can't retire; he has a small amount of money left, but he's probably always going to have to work.

In that situation, some people might express **frustration**. People always complain, but what does it get them? Life throws curveballs. Herbert may not have always done the right thing, but instead of focusing on what's been taken from him, he concentrates on what he has. He has a home. He's paid off his credit card debt. He still gets to hunt and ice fish all winter. Now he's rebuilding his relationship with his daughter and beginning a new role as a grandfather. He's found contentment with the life he has.

Throughout your life, you may encounter challenges that keep you from thriving, as you'd wish to. You may be ahead on your mortgage when, all of a sudden, a big medical bill comes in. You may not be able to take a vacation every year; you may not be able to leave a big nest egg behind for your kids. But no matter your situation, you can control the mind-set with which you approach it. Herbert's story shows that it's possible to be happy no matter what happens.

*Sometimes, people in more **secure** positions than Herbert can't accept that they're stable enough to retire and enjoy* *their time. In* **security**, *people who have done a good job saving and preparing still look at their accounts and think, I could've done more. They wish they were leaving more money for their heirs, or they want to be able to take more vacations. They hem and haw over things they could have, would have, or wish they'd done.*

Hindsight is 20/20, but you can't change the past. You can only look to the future. People who have **security** *of mind-set may have the money to do something like take a vacation, but they don't believe it. They're good planners, so they feel nervous about spending. But think about your purpose in retirement: Is it better to live more conservatively than necessary, or to make the best of your time?*

People in **security** *often have the money to spend, but they don't believe they can spend it. That's where financial planning comes in: a good financial advisor can help you spend responsibly to take advantage of everything you've saved for. Life will still throw you curveballs, but if your emergency fund is stocked and you're insulated against uncertainties, there's no reason not to use what you have.*

GRACE'S STORY: MAXIMIZING TRIUMPH

Grace planned well and lives frugally, but she still has trouble believing that she can afford any kind of luxuries.

Grace is eighty-four; she and her husband, Perry, had been married for almost sixty years when he passed away five years go. For years and years they'd lived thriftily, never taking on more debt than they could handle, always making sure their kids had what they needed.

Until he died, Perry had always been the one to handle the family's finances. Grace managed the pocketbook expenses, but Perry had a view of the big picture. Because he felt comfortable with that, and Grace trusted her husband, the two of them rarely discussed what was going on in their accounts. They lived within their means, and that was enough.

Grace and Perry had a son and a daughter. Both of them got excellent educations and went into lucrative careers, but they also struggled mightily in their lives. As a result, Perry had always made sure that he and Grace were able to help them out of jams when necessary. It wasn't something they talked much about, just something Perry took care of.

When Perry died, he and Grace were in good financial shape. Thanks to his planning, Grace and their children would have the assets for whatever they needed. But because he didn't want Grace to worry, he never talked to her about their portfolio. He simply told her, "It'll all be all right."

That reassurance was enough when Perry was alive and Grace could hear it straight from him, but things changed when he was no longer around. Left with a few inheritances and various accounts to manage, Grace felt overwhelmed. Her daughter, Maude, a health-policy researcher, knew that her mother needed guidance. It wasn't that Grace didn't have the money; it was that she didn't know how her money could work for her. Maude had to help her mother understand what was going on and how flexible she truly was.

Back in the days when Grace and Perry were raising their family, they didn't have much money. Then, right around the time when they retired, one of their relatives died and left them a large lump sum. Even so, they continued drawing the same amount from their accounts as they'd always planned to. They had no debt, they always paid their bills, and they just wanted to live as they always had. But after Perry died and Grace began looking at their portfolio, she wanted to find ways to help their children through some truly trying times.

Their children struggled. Their son Josh had a hard time finding his way; he'd tried his hand as an entrepreneur, but he couldn't quite make things work. At one point, he even moved back in with his parents for a couple of years. Still, Grace and Perry voiced their support and never let their Josh's business failures affect their relationship with him. They kept encouraging him, making sure he knew that he had their unconditional love and support.

Although Maude was successful in her career, she was having a very difficult time at home. She'd married young and had two children, and her husband had stayed home with the kids while she pursued her career. That was fine—for a time. But then, just before Perry died, Maude found out that her husband had been having an affair. She was devastated, but for a long time, she didn't tell her parents what was going on. She didn't want to worry them when her father was sick. Her husband assured her that the affair was over and he was ready to repair the damage that had been done to their marriage.

Grace appreciated all her daughter's help, but she was worried. Maude was behaving strangely. With her son off pursuing a new business interest, Grace's daughter was the one helping her mother go through her father's things and set up financial allotments as needed. Maude was normally a punctual person, but she kept showing up late to scheduled meetings and events. It seemed like there was more going on than just the grief of losing her father.

Eventually Grace confronted her daughter, who broke down and told her mother that, although she thought her husband had ended his affair, she'd discovered messages from his mistress on his phone. Now she couldn't trust her husband at all. She was sure their marriage was over.

Grace supported Maude emotionally, spending more time with her and helping out with her grandchildren so that her daughter and son-in-law could go to counseling. But things didn't improve.

When Maude finally went to a lawyer to begin the process of filing for divorce, she got some terrible news. The lawyers told her that if she left her husband, he'd get to take 50 percent of their assets. Even though he had been unfaithful, that was how the laws in their state worked. Maude is accomplished in her field, but she's not a high earner; if she lost 50 percent of her assets, she wouldn't be able to afford a place to live with enough room for the kids. And so, for now, she has to stay with her unfaithful husband. It's a terrible situation.

Grace wanted to help her daughter in any way she could. However, she knew that if she gave Maude money, there was a chance it could end up in her son-in-law's hands. She needed information, so she did some research and learned that because she hadn't been taking her required minimum distribution, her children would owe significant taxes when she passed away. She began drawing more from her account, and through further research she learned how she could set up trusts for her daughter and her grandchildren—accounts that only they could access after her death. Once she saw that she was in a position of real *security*, she found that she would be able to help her loved ones.

Despite the obstacles that Grace has faced, she's a cheerful, upbeat person. She was nervous about her accounts at first, but now that she knows her bequest can make her children's lives easier, she's taken a more active role in management. Even though she hates the feeling of drawing extra money out of an account, she sees the constructive purpose of setting up accounts for her children and grandchildren.

Once Grace had been working on her trusts for a couple of years and building her confidence, she began thinking of other ways that she could leave a legacy. She truly believed in her ability to touch others' lives through her attitude and actions. Over the last three years, Grace has quietly begun to establish a series of trusts, not only for her family, but also for organizations dear to her. Because she has a strong financial foundation and a positive mind-set about everything she's gone through, Grace has been able to transcend her circumstances and make more of an impact than she would've thought possible. Even though her children are still struggling, Grace is buoyed by the knowledge that her bequest will help them and others in her community live life to the fullest. "I know that everything's going to be okay," she says.

It can be difficult to consider how your mind-set is affecting how you live and how you approach your retirement. Sometimes it's hard even to see how your attitude affects the other aspects of your life. When push comes to shove, the way you live comes down to the way you see the world.

Whether you think you can or you think you can't, you're right. Now that you've read Grace and Herbert's story, you can see how attitude controls your ability to affect the world around you. It takes money, but it's not about the money. Whether you're a high earner with a big nest egg or a blue-collar worker on a frugal retirement plan, if you have the right mind-set, everything will work out.

Using the scorecard below, rate yourself on your mind-set when it comes to retirement.

PERSONAL SCORE CARD – *Eight Things I Wish I Knew Before I Retired*

Mindset	IDEAL	REAL		
		So Not Me	I'm Working Toward	You Know Me So Well
I have planned for the unexpected and I don't sweat the small things.		☐	☐	☐

A SEND-OFF

AFTER THE PARTY, BOB FEELS GRATIFIED. HE CAN'T believe how many people showed up just to wish him well. As he and his wife, Betty, exit his office building, Bob feels a circle of care surrounding him. While there are still pieces of retirement to figure out, he knows that with the support of his friends and family, everything will turn out just fine.

When Bob and Betty walk out into the parking lot, Bob's uncle Harvey is waiting for them. Harvey drove in just for the retirement party. Harvey's in his eighties, and he's a true inspiration for Bob, who has long admired his work ethic, his genial outlook on life, and—most of all—the way he's given back to his family and community in his golden years while still growing as a person. While Bob would never try to make a big deal out of his milestone, Betty made sure that Harvey was here for this celebration.

"How about some dinner?" Harvey asks.

Bob looks to Betty, who says, "We already made a reservation at your favorite place."

Bob is stunned. He's still overwhelmed by all the effort everyone has put in to recognize him.

He and Betty walk to their car and follow Harvey to the restaurant. When they arrive, the host seats the three of them at their favorite table, where they have plenty of privacy to laugh and chat. As they enjoy a round of appetizers, Harvey begins to reminisce about Bob's earlier years.

He says, "I remember when you were leaving for college. You were so anxious! You were leaving home for the first time, and even though your mother had made sure you had all the things you needed, you kept thinking that something was missing. And today, at your send-off party, you kept asking people for advice."

Bob shakes his head and chuckles a little bit.

"I thought I had to have everything figured out right away."

Betty nods in agreement and says, "I remember feeling like that when I started my first job. I thought that if I made a mistake, even a small one, everything would come crashing down around me. I was sure I was doomed."

Now Bob begins to laugh out loud, his laughter resounding throughout the restaurant. Heads turn, but he doesn't care. He's been so stressed, and what for? He's survived other life changes; retirement will surely be a challenge, but one he can meet with the skills he already has.

"Bob, I know you can handle this next step," says Harvey, "but I want you to have a professional on your side. Give The Tranel Financial Group a call. They can help give you the clarity and confidence you're looking for."

Harvey opens his wallet and pulls out a business card, sliding it across the table to Bob.

"Thanks, Uncle Harvey," says Bob. "I think I'm ready to make that call."

*Eight Things I Wish
I Knew Before I Retired*

IDEAL VERSUS REAL

Retirement brings out many emotions relating to your new purpose in life and your new retired identity. Look for the Personal Score Card at the end of each chapter, and tally them using the full Personal Score Card at the back of the book. This is an excellent tool that you can use to navigate the road of retirement.

The statements are designed to highlight areas that need further attention and development. Our goal is to help you identify the key components of your dream retirement plan.

Find Out Your Score NOW! »

PERSONAL SCORE CARD – *Eight Things I Wish I Knew Before I Retired*

IDEAL   REAL

Mindset	So Not Me	I'm Working Toward	You Know Me So Well
I measure my purpose through my growth, and through my impact on myself, my community and the world.	☐	☐	☐
Work is just a small part of who I am. I identify myself through my hobbies and my happiness.	☐	☐	☐
I am at peace and happy where I am in life. I rarely think about money, knowing I am in a good place.	☐	☐	☐
Days don't always go as planned, but I have a great life plan to allow for ups and downs.	☐	☐	☐

Mindset	So Not Me	I'm Working Toward	You Know Me So Well
I have dealt with the reality of life, and I am leaving behind a legacy I am proud of.	☐	☐	☐
My plan is working, and allows me to live a stress-free lifestyle with clarity and independence.	☐	☐	☐
Being debt-free allows me to live confidently in a world that is ever changing.	☐	☐	☐
I have planned for the unexpected and I don't sweat the small things.	☐	☐	☐
Column Totals:	☐	☐	☐

Eight Things I Wish I Knew Before I Retired
Your RESULTS

IF YOU SCORED THE MOST IN

So Not Me

It sounds like life may be happening to you, rather than the other way around. Possibly your work is your identity, but despite all your hard work, you are uncertain about your future. A Discovery meeting and a good financial plan can help you to dream about the future, make plans, and retire with confidence.

IF YOU SCORED THE MOST IN

I'm Working Toward

You know retirement is important, and you are doing some planning for the future. Work is very much a part of your identity, and although you do have a retirement plan in place, you wish you could do more. You feel you may be missing something. We would ask, "What are your big, audacious goals?" A competent financial advisor could guide you to financial clarity, and the insight you are looking for.

IF YOU SCORED THE MOST IN

You Know Me So Well

Congratulations! You have planned well for retirement. You feel good about what you have accomplished, and you have thought out your future well. You are always open to learning, and you stay informed about wealth and finance. A relationship with a knowledgeable financial advisor can help you continue to "Enjoy a Better Life."

138

ABOUT THE AUTHORS

Roch Tranel, Certified Financial Planner, is CEO and founder of The Tranel Financial Group located in Libertyville, Illinois. Roch has been helping individuals reach clarity and confidence about their financial future for over 25 years. Helping people *Enjoy a Better Life* through successful financial planning is Roch's passion in life. Roch has assembled a team of professional financial advisors who are committed to the same principles and share the same commitment to providing an unparalleled client experience.

As an active leader in his community, Roch has served on several boards, including the GLMV Chamber, The Rotary Club, and the Great Lakes Adaptive Sports Association and Pinnacle Forum. Currently Roch is President of Founders 55

NFP, Inc. where he enjoys using his gifts of innovation and leadership. He also shares these gifts by supporting The Global Leadership Summit, Freedom One Networking and the Taste of Life Intern Program at The Tranel Financial Group.

Roch is the author of three books, *The Friend Economy* and *Sunny Side Up*, along with his new book, *Eight Things I Wish I Knew Before I Retired*.

Roch resides in Libertyville, Illinois, with his wife, Kathleen, and their children, Jenna and Alec.

———

Tyler Braun is a financial advisor with the Tranel Financial Group. Tyler has a true passion for helping people through all phases of life. Since joining the Tranel Financial Group, he has helped thousands of people through the retirement process and into their retirement years. Tyler takes pride in the relationships he cultivates with his clients, and feels that they are part of his family.

Tyler is very excited about his first book, which he has co-authored with Roch Tranel, and he is confident that it will be of great value to readers in their retirement planning.

Tyler resides in Bristol, Wisconsin, with his wife, Amber, and their children, Carter and Tatum.

He enjoys the outdoors, spending time with his family, and serving others.

Made in the USA
Columbia, SC
14 April 2019